CULTIVATING

the inner life

A Guide to Spiritual Practices
that Nurture the Soul

Terri White

Fourth Edition

Cultivating the Inner Life: A Guide to Spiritual Practices that Nurture the Soul
Fourth Edition

Unless otherwise indicated, Scripture quotations are taken from the New International Version.

Additional copies may be ordered from:

Terri White
P.O. Box 786
Corvallis, OR 97330

The following graphics must be credited as follows:

- Man plowing — IMSI's MasterClips/MasterPhotos Collection, 1895 Francisco Blvd, East, San Rafael, CA 94901-5506, USA
- Vine — © [Imagination13] / Adobe Stock

ISBN 13: 979-8-218-60448-6
ISBN 10: 8-218-60448-6

ACKNOWLEDGEMENTS

To Tom, my husband, my best friend, mentor and closest spiritual companion on life's journey. Your walk with the Lord has truly shaped my life and soul. You obediently "keep your hand on the plow," persevering and wholeheartedly pursuing the Lord and attentively shepherding others with His healing love. Thank you for inspiring and encouraging me to persevere and update this book after twenty years. What a joy working on it together!

To Cynthia Leonard, close friend and ministry colleague, who patiently and lovingly did edits and formatting for all editions of this book. This would not be in your hands without Cynthia!

TABLE OF CONTENTS

PREFACE

For my determined purpose is that I may know Him, that I may progressively become more deeply and intimately acquainted with Him, perceiving and recognizing and understanding the wonders of His person more strongly and more clearly. And that I may in that same way come to know the power outflowing from His resurrection and that I may so share in His sufferings **as to be continually transformed in Spirit into His likeness,** *even to His death.*

—Philippians 3:10 (Amplified)

Since the first days of my walk with Jesus this passage has captured and summarized all I have longed for! Throughout the years my one passion and determined purpose has been to know Him more intimately. For me, it has been a daily journey filled with questions and discovery as how to *practically* walk out this purpose in my life.

How do I cultivate my inner life? What does the Lord require of me? Does it matter how often or how long my quiet times should be? How do I become transformed into His likeness? How do I continually abide, keeping a continuous exchange of love between me and my Lord amidst the noise, the voices, and busy-ness of life? Is it simply enough "just to love Him," or am I to be more intentional in this love relationship? How do I love Him with all my heart, mind, soul and strength, so my whole being is centered on Him? Why are the disciplines at times so seemingly hard to practice? Are they truly essential for spiritual growth?

I have not found neat, "packaged" answers to all my questions. But I *have* learned one important truth in my journey seeking God. Everything I do in pursuing Him—even asking these questions—must be rooted in this one, determined purpose...*to know Him.* And I come to know Him by being **with Him.** And the more I am with Him, the more I learn to **hear Him** speaking personally to me.

I titled this book "Cultivating the Inner Life" for a reason. This booklet is really about pursuing and coming to know Him by *making space* in our lives to meet Him in spiritual practices and prayers of the heart. What is the essence of these practices? *We are cultivating a listening heart!* If our pursuit is to know Him, we need to learn how to recognize our Shepherd's voice. Jesus states a profound truth: "My sheep hear my voice, and I know them, and they follow Me..." You *can* learn and be trained to hear His sacred voice of truth! Spiritual practices position us to hear His voice. This is how we build personal relationship with our Lord and cultivate our inner lives. We will explore these practices, and as we do, let's come with receptive hearts, as young Samuel did, "Speak, Lord, your servant is listening."

As I have cultivated my inner life through the practice of the spiritual disciplines, I have found that I must do them out of a sincerity of *desire,* from an obedience inspired and motivated by love for Him, and the experiential knowledge that I am truly anchored in His love. It is only *that* kind of obedience, rooted in this truth, that has enabled me to daily practice them in spite of my feelings, seasons in the wilderness, difficult trials, and often the mundane, ordinary days of life.

Numerous times, Jesus said to His disciples, "Come away with me" (Mark 6:31-33). What a profound invitation from the God of the universe! He wants to be *with* you! He desires and waits for you to come, because He wants to speak to you! As you come, it is important to remember the truth that He made you in His image. You are unique (fearfully and wonderfully made, Psalm 139). There has never been another you in the history of mankind, and there never will be! You have a place of delight and joy in God's heart that no one has, or ever will have. The Lord not only wants you to learn to hear *His* voice. He is also fully attentive to *you.* He calls you by name and hears *your* voice distinct from all others. David, a man after God's own heart, wrote:

In my distress, I called to the Lord.
I cried to my God for help,and He heard my voice out of His temple.
My cry came before Him into His ears.
—Psalm 18:6

The Lord, who knows you, wants to make Himself known to you as El Roi, the Lord who *sees* you...as Immanuel, the Lord *with* you...as Jehovah Rohi, the Lord, your Shepherd, who *speaks* to your soul! You are seen, known and loved unconditionally. That is the joy of pursuing Him!

As you pick up and put to use the cultivating tools in this booklet, my prayer is that your quiet times will become a sacred dwelling place, a transforming encounter with your Lord, as you increasingly experience His personal acceptance, and hear Him call you by name, His beloved.

He is longing and waiting for you to come... to meet Him...just as you are.

May you delight in Him as you journey on.

Terri

A WELL-WATERED GARDEN

As I ponder "cultivating the inner life," there's a beautiful metaphor in Isaiah 58:11 that vividly describes the Lord's heart and purpose for His people:

The Lord will guide you always. He will satisfy your needs in a sun-scorched land and will strengthen your frame. You will be like a well-watered garden, like a spring of water that never fails.

This metaphor of a well-watered, cultivated garden is a frame for the content and focus of this book. He alone can make my sun-scorched soul into a well-watered garden. He is the source of a perpetual spring within me—of refreshment, inner strength and fruitfulness. But this requires that *I tend to the soil of my soul.* It is imperative that I notice, pay attention to, and nurture my inner life.

In keeping connected to the Lord, the most important step is to awaken each day with our heart and mind inclined to listen for and notice His sacred voice of truth, intentionally making space to be *with* Him.

Here's a personal prayer He gave me that I often daily offer to the Lord:

"I want to be present in your presence."

What does it look like in my life to pay attention to and tend to the soil of my soul? How do I "practice presence?" How do I cultivate a listening heart? How can I spend increased time with Him to better hear the voice of my Shepherd speaking to my soul?

Psalm 131 is written by David, a Psalm of Ascent, an outpouring of a singular desire to seek the presence of the Lord. These profound words of a shepherd boy turned king have been a *soul guide* for me as I learn how to live out this desire.

As a king, imagine David dealing daily with numerous demands, duties and endless responsibilities. Like you and me, he must have been pulled in many directions, constantly distracted. But notice these astounding words:

My heart is not proud Lord, my eyes are not haughty.
I do not concern myself with great matters or
things too wonderful for me. But I have calmed and quieted myself.
I am like a weaned child with its mother. Like a weaned child, I am
content. Israel, put your hope in the Lord now and forever.

Here are David's words in a modern paraphrase (the Message)

God, I am not trying to rule the roost, I don't want to be king of the
mountain. I haven't meddled where I have no business or fantasized
grandiose plans. I've kept my feet on the ground, I've cultivated a
quiet heart. Like a baby content in its mother's arms, my soul is a baby
content. Wait, Israel, for God. Wait with hope. Hope now; hope always!

Through the years I've found myself returning to and pondering these specific words: ***I have calmed and quieted myself. I have cultivated a quiet heart.***

Yes, this is a deep longing of my soul. To walk with the Lord in such a way through the ebbs and flows of life, my soul remains in that quiet, restful place, like the weaned child. A place of settled rest, peacefulness, not striving or demanding, just being content—as a beloved child being held by its mother.

I like how the Message captures David's mindset: "I've kept my boots on the ground. I've cultivated a quiet heart." This is the image of where we live. We all walk and live in the trenches (the war zones) of the real world! But here's the question—in the midst of the messes, stresses and sorrows of life, how do we gain and maintain a quiet heart?

Clearly, David's secret was that he cultivated a quiet, attentive heart towards the Lord. Soul soil needs to be well cultivated to bring forth the best growth. It must be thoroughly worked—uprooting old root systems and breaking the soil till the spade can easily go in, and seeds can be planted.

How did David cultivate? This is what I perceive or imagine about him as I meditate on his psalms and his life. He was intentional taking time to slow down, to stop, to invite the Lord to speak to him. Then we hear him speaking to his own soul, ***"Be still...be quiet my soul."***

He speaks to the condition of his soul: his racing mind, his up and down

A WELL-WATERED GARDEN

moods, his physical impulses. "Quiet down!" He chose to do this, so he could hear and discern His voice distinct from his own. This is something we do. This is our part. He was intentional to listen for God's voice even in the midst of his busy life. He says, my soul "waits on God." So he made space for silence and solitude, letting the Lord interrupt his cycles of busyness. He gave the Lord access to his heart. He brought everything to God in prayer, even the dark, struggling parts. He humbly cries out for deeper intimacy. We hear his longings, failures, anguish, disappointments, perplexities and joys. *We see in his life a continual seeking, returning to and focusing on the Lord.* This was his one pursuit.

As David made space in the moments of life to pause, to become self-aware of his actions and reactions, we hear his responses of confession, forgiveness, thanksgiving. Taking time to pause and notice the movements of his inner life allowed the Lord by His Spirit to transform David's internal responses and perspectives of his daily activities, interactions with people, weighty decisions. *He gave the Lord permission to cultivate his soul soil. His life became a well-watered garden. A continual spring.*

Let me share this small but significant example. One morning, as I was awakening, I stretched my hand to my bed-stand, where my phone was, and I heard the Lord say, "Reach for me first, before you reach for the phone." That got my attention! Since then I put my phone at night in another room, and I now awaken with my eyes and gaze first on Him! The Lord notices and delights in the slightest heart movements toward Him as I allow Him to cultivate my soil. *One small step can change the trajectory of my soul!*

I have found cultivating to be a continual process. This is not a one-time or one-off thing. This was David's secret to being a man after God's own heart. This is how he kept company with *his* King!

David also knew the profound truth that the Lord was an *invitational* God!

In Psalm 27:8 (New Living Translation) he writes:

Lord, my heart has heard you say, "come talk to me," and my heart responds, Lord, I am coming!

I'd like to point out something significant here. In Psalm 131 we notice David being intentional to "quiet" his soul. Why? So that he can better distinguish God's voice from the constant flow of thoughts and voices going on in his

II

life. Notice also in Psalm 27, David hears the Lord speaking, "Come talk to me!" *A quieted heart is a heart poised to be a listening heart.* So, one of the core reasons for practicing the spiritual disciplines is to learn to discern and better hear the voice of our Shepherd guiding and empowering our lives.

We see in Isaiah a profound description of this intentionality of a servant of the Lord to hear and submit to God's word:

The Sovereign Lord has given me an instructed tongue,
To know the word that sustains the weary.
He wakens me morning by morning,
Wakens my ear to listen like one being taught.
The Sovereign Lord has opened my ears,
And I have not been rebellious;
I have not drawn back.

—Isaiah 50:4, 5

Morning by morning, day by day, the Lord invites me to *come… and keep coming…and keep listening.* Sometimes I imagine Him in the morning, saying, "Wake up, Terri. I can't wait to tell you something!" He wants intimacy with us. As we come, *He meets us where we are, not where we should be.* He is in the midst of all that concerns us, and every circumstance of our lives! This is profoundly personal.

May the Lord teach us how to build rhythms and make space to be present in His presence. *We want to learn how to let Him tend to and nurture our souls, so we can be a well-watered garden, with inner springs of His life flowing daily into and out of our inner lives.*

Take an unhurried moment. Quiet your heart and read Psalm 131. Notice how the Lord is getting your attention. Listen for gentle, inner whispers of His voice. Envision what your soul as a well-watered garden could look like.

CULTIVATING
THE INNER LIFE

Jesus told this parable: A farmer went out to sow His seed. As he was scattering the seed some fell along the path; it was trampled on, and the birds of the air ate it up. Some fell on rock, and when it came up the plants withered because they had no moisture. Other seed fell among thorns, which grew up with it and choked the plants. Still other seed fell on good soil. It came up and yielded a crop, a hundred times more than was sown.

This is the meaning of the parable: The seed is the word of God. Those along the path are the ones who hear, and then the devil comes and takes away the word from their hearts, so that they may not believe and be saved. Those on the rock are the ones who receive the word with joy when they hear it, but they have no root. They believe for a while, but in the time of testing they fall away. The seed that fell among the thorns stands for those who hear, but as they go on their way they are choked by life's worries, riches, and pleasures, and they do not mature. But the seed on good soil stands for those with a noble and good heart, who hear the word, retain it, and by persevering produce a crop.

—Luke 8:4-15

In the last section, we explored the metaphor of a fruitful life being "a well-watered garden." We looked briefly at David's singular intention to still and quiet his soul, his resolve to "cultivate the soil of his heart."

As we're looking at the components of "cultivating the inner life," I'd like to carry this imagery into the New Testament. Jesus, the master storyteller, used contrast to make truth come to life. This parable about the seed and condition of soil can be applied on many levels. Yes, He is describing the different ways unbelievers respond to hearing truth. But for those with a "noble and good heart," the seed goes into soul soil that has been prepared and cultivated, open to receive and retain the seed, producing the fruit of spiritual maturity.

There are so many times when I reflect on areas of my life that require change. In those moments, I long too often for a quick fix, an easy path or a growth spurt! But *I was reminded one day just how slow a process growth really is.* As I entered my laundry room, my eye caught the growth marks on the wall we had made for our children each year. It was always such fun for them to measure their growth, sometimes month by month, but for them it was never fast enough!

Yet for us as parents the greater joy was found in moments we "saw" marks of the inner growth of character and maturity in their lives. Even though our children are out of the nest now, we continue to process the "miracle" of their growth (and ours) in areas we never imagined. But we also discern areas where further maturity is needed. We are a people in process. Maturity requires intentionality on our part, and takes time. Our God is understanding and patient. He responds when we express willingness to change, and desire to grow.

What does it mean to cultivate? Webster defines it this way: "to prepare and use the soil; to till; to break up surface soil around plants in order to destroy weeds and preserve moisture; to grow plants from seeds and buds." From Jesus' parable we see that the word of God sometimes fell on poor heart soil...full of rocks and thorns that prevented the seed from taking root and coming to maturity. The soil needed to be cultivated. *Practicing such spiritual disciplines as prayer, meditation, and solitude gets the seed of truth into the soil of our hearts.* The good soil received the seed of truth, was able to retain it, persevere (continue in spite of obstacles, steadfast in purpose), and produce fruit. The seed took root! Therefore, it's important to "humbly accept the word planted in you" (James 1:21). That's the kind of "heart soil" I want to cultivate in my life!

Where does this kind of growth really occur? In the roots of my soul. Roots are defined as "a part of a plant below the ground that lacks nodes, shoots and leaves, and holds the plant in position; draws water and nourishment from the soil and stores food." Spiritually, when I am born again, God implants in me the seed of a whole new nature (1 Peter 1:23). This is a supernatural impartation of His Holy Spirit that is both glorious and mysterious. There are, then, new roots that need nurture, new shoots that need care. But there are also the old roots all tangled up in the impulses of my old life, all the self-centeredness that Paul calls "the flesh." Following my new birth in Christ, justification, I start the lifelong process of sanctification, in which God releases divine power to dig up and put to death the old roots and empowers the new roots of my new nature to take hold. It is amazing to me that it is in this place of the heart where all is concealed, dark, unseen and unnoticed by others, where God gently brings me to points of *confrontation* (exposing my old self) and *consecration* (yielding myself to Him to strengthen my new nature and produce the character of His Son in me). Only the Father, my master Gardener, sees those seeds and roots embedded in the self-willed soil of my old nature. As I choose to admit and confess these roots of unbelief, self-centeredness, bitterness, anger, envy, jealousy, He provides holy power in my inner life to both wither away the power of sin, and water the roots of my new nature (humility, gentleness, selfless love, etc.). *His life continually in me replaces my old life.*

Without a good root system we lose moisture. Our faith dries up. We risk spiritual death. We can only give an appearance of godliness for so long (looking like a healthy plant but lacking good roots). *But our roots always reveal our true condition.* As our roots become strong through regular nourishment and tests and trials, they bring stability to our lives and enable us to stand against the winds of the world, the flesh, and the devil. They hold us in position!

If we are *faithful* to daily cultivate and nourish the roots (the depth) and soil of our hearts, then He will take care of the height and breadth of our lives (the fruit-blossoms, the works of salvation). You see, *Faithfulness leads to fruitfulness!*

Jeremiah expressed it this way:

Blessed is the man who trusts in the Lord, whose confidence is in Him. He will be like a tree planted by the water that sends out its roots by the stream. It does not fear when heat comes; its leaves are always green. It has no worries in a year of drought and never fails to bear fruit.
—Jeremiah 17:7,8

Don't you long to be that kind of tree, with deep roots and abundant fruits? Your heart does not fear when you hear bad news. You do not wither away and weaken through the daily trials and tests, but stay green and nourished, and you flourish. And when others are worrying about resources being depleted, you know who supplies your root system with water they know not of...and you always bear the fruit of the Spirit in and out of season because you are attentive to your inner life and relationship with Him.

Cultivating the inner life requires continuing desire, commitment, discipline, and perseverance. There are no shortcuts or easy paths. And the process sometimes seems slow. Psalm 37:3 (NASB) says, *"Dwell in the land and cultivate faithfulness." This is a picture of us daily, faithfully and intentionally keeping our hand to the plow.* In the pages ahead, we will discover some of the tools required for cultivating the kind of soil that produces intimacy with Him and fruit that blesses others around us.

Sow for yourselves righteousness, reap the fruit of unfailing love, and break up your unplowed ground, for it is time to seek the Lord until he comes and showers righteousness on you.

—Hosea 10:12

Taking Time to Reflect

1. Reflecting on the content of this chapter, take a personal "soil sample." How would you describe the current condition of your inner life? Is your soil receptive to seed? Hardened? Stony, in need of cultivation? Any thorns (anything that chokes out the seed)? Perhaps a word picture comes to mind that describes where you are. Spend some time right now getting specific with the Lord in prayer about the condition of your soul.

2. How are you noticing God maturing you?

3. Re-visit the Lord's promise revealed in Jeremiah 17:7,8. Take some time to personalize this by praying through the Scripture, expressing your own desire for increased fruitfulness, making this promise your own.

RESTING IN GOD

Before we look at understanding and practicing the spiritual disciplines, I want to explore the Lord's consistent invitation throughout Scripture to those who follow Him, to come into a place of true soul rest. We begin in Psalm 84, looking at the picture of Israel's pilgrimage from places of stress, to the place of rest in His presence.

Blessed are those whose strength is in you,
who have set their hearts on pilgrimage
[in whose hearts are the highways].
As they pass through the valley of Baca [weeping],
they make it a place of springs;
the autumn rains also cover it with pools.
They go from strength to strength,
till each appears before God in Zion.

—Psalm 84: 5-7

For the old-covenant Jew, the call to come up to Jerusalem to observe a feast meant travel... often through dry, difficult and dangerous places. But the privilege of connecting with God Himself provided the motivation and courage to make these journeys. The Hebrew language literally describes the pilgrim attitude this way: "in whose hearts are the highways." *In other words, making the effort to travel to meet with God was an internal, unquenchable passion.* **Their hearts were set on pilgrimage.** *Any obstacle could be overcome.*

As new covenant Christians, we are also called to pilgrimage. We are each on our own unique journey with the Lord individually, and as a Church corporately. In this fallen and alien world, we must travel through a variety of terrain... mountains, caves, dark valleys, narrow places, meadows, deserts, occasional oases, thick forests, rocky crags, etc. We also experience different seasons of life and discover within ourselves many areas of need: a crossroads where we need direction, times when we cry out for strength and patience to persevere, seasons of lament or grieving, times when we need faith to trust. We may face hunger, thirst, longing for companionship, gripping fear, worry, and restlessness.

When overcome with inevitable weariness, our hearts identify with the Psalmist: "My soul finds rest in God alone" (62:1). My natural self will always cry out for rest and earthly sustenance. I seek for a break in the routine, "rest stops" to get replenished, yet I still find myself restless. But our Lord continually offers us a rest that is inexhaustible. He supplies what we lack. He enables us to keep moving from strength to strength until we meet Him face to face in Zion.

We hear this invitation for spiritual rest in the prophetic words of Isaiah. He clearly points to the source of rest, but is quick to rebuke Israel for her refusal to "go there!"

This is what the Sovereign Lord, the Holy One of Israel says:
"In repentance and rest is your salvation,
in quietness and trust is your strength,
but you would have none of it."
—Isaiah 30:15

Jesus offers a similar invitation:

Come to me [keep on coming!] all you who are weary and burdened, and
I will give you rest.
Take my yoke upon you and learn from me,
for I am gentle and humble in heart,
and you will find rest for your souls.
—Matthew 11:28, 29

I love the paraphrase of Jesus' remarkable invitation in the Message:

Are you tired? Worn out? Burned out on religion?
Come to me. Get away with me and you'll discover your life.
I'll show you how to take a real rest.
Walk with me and work with me—watch how I do it.
Learn the unforced rhythms of grace.
I won't lay anything heavy or ill-fitting on you.
Keep company with me and you'll learn to live freely and lightly.

So where and how do we find true rest? With the stressful pace of life today, this is a real question. *The Lord alone is our rest.* What does this mean? It means that He alone can satisfy the deepest longings of our souls. It means that we have the choice to seek Him as our true Source, to come to Him in faith to be enabled to release the tension of our self-directed ways and submit to *His* ways. "Come to me... and you will find rest for your souls." *The language here depicts an admission of our exhaustion and the action to decide to come. Jesus wants you and me to learn that the source of our life and our strength is in Him alone.*

Is this where you'd like to be in your inner life? Let's go a bit further understanding how to experience the rest God offers. The writer to the Hebrews shares an historic object lesson:

So, as the Holy Spirit says, "Today, if you hear his voice,
do not harden your hearts as you did in the rebellion,
during the time of testing in the desert,
where your fathers tested and tried me for forty years and saw what I did.
That is why I was angry with that generation, and I said,
'Their hearts are always going astray,
and they have not known my ways.
So I declared an oath in my anger,
They shall never enter my rest.'"

—Hebrews 3:7-11

How do we understand "rest" in the Hebrew mindset? The meaning is to settle down, cease from labor. The word picture is the releasing of the tension of cords that have been tightly wound and woven. So, some kind of inappropriate activity or tension in my inner life must come to an end, and a discipline of releasing and resting begin. I stop what I am doing and surrender. And through that surrender and releasing comes true rest. This is totally contrary to how we are wired ("they go astray in their hearts").

Let us therefore be zealous and exert ourselves and strive diligently to
enter into that rest—to know and experience it for ourselves—
that no one may fall or perish by the same kind of unbelief and
disobedience (into which those in the wilderness fell).

—Hebrews 4:11 (Amplified Bible)

"Exert ourselves and strive diligently" to experience spiritual rest? How does **that** work? It is vital that we understand this. We exert ourselves in several ways:

- Seeking to know God personally and intimately for who He is
- Practicing spiritual disciplines and prayers of the heart
- Saturating my soul in His Word
- Taking small steps to build Sabbath into my life
- Understanding His ways, how He relates to me, how He speaks, disciplines, and empowers me

As I humbly seek Him with a hungry heart and build the spiritual disciplines into my walk, they become a pathway to experience true soul rest. As I learn to dwell on the beauty of His character and attributes, I open my inner life to Him, submit to His dealings with me, and relinquish my fleshly strivings. *I must come to see that I **cannot** and **will not** produce authentic spiritual rest.* I must come to the Maker and Master, give up my own restless ways, lie down, and receive. What an incredible exchange—my striving for His shalom (peace, well-being, wholeness), my anxious activity for the empowerment of His Spirit. God waits to turn my tears to trust and my fears to faith *if* I will simply let Him!

The dreadful alternative is a hardening of heart (petrified, emotionally indifferent, calloused). A hardened heart has chosen to recoil from intimacy and to refuse trust. Unbelief leads to a distancing from our true Source and a deadening of the inner life.

The invitation is open, and the alternative painfully clear. There seems to be such simplicity in choosing to trust and to come. But here's the rub—the human heart is prone to perpetual self-reliance and stubbornness. This is the main point of the Hebrews object lesson. Watch out! Don't make the same mistake. Guard your inner heart response to the Lord! "Today [every day] if you hear his voice, do not harden your heart."

Responding to a call to cultivate disciplines that shape our interior lives is really about first being honest about our disillusionment and exhaustion with all the outer things we do and responding to Jesus' invitation to come to Him to find the real Source of our life and purpose. We are fashioned in the very image and likeness of the Father, Son, and Holy Spirit. We are designed to find our true home, a place of peace, rest and purpose, in the presence of our triune God. He has provided, in both Old and New Covenant revelation, a map to find our way home.

In your own heart, are you traveling the "highways" that lead to His Presence? Are the signposts clear to you as you're traveling? Let's explore briefly what these spiritual disciplines are, and how we are to practice them in the context of everyday life. His invitation is clear: *"Come unto me..."*

Dear reader, I encourage you to remember who you are coming to—Jesus is a gentle, caring Shepherd, humble in heart. He will not lay anything heavy on you.

Take my yoke upon you
...and you will find rest for your souls.

Taking Time to Reflect

1. Take a few minutes and think of some ways you could build spiritual rest into your life.

2. Think through the flow of your life over the past 30 days. Identify specific things that seem to regularly rob you of spiritual rest. Where does your heart go astray? What short-circuits God's provision of peace (mental and emotional well-being)? Are there areas of stress or tension that you need to identify and release to God?

3. Jesus invites those weary and burdened to "come" to Him for rest. What, specifically, wearies or burdens you? Are you ready to respond to Jesus' invitation to come to Him as the only one who can provide you with true spiritual rest? If "yes," then "come" now in prayer, and process with the Lord what you've discovered about yourself in the exercise above.

OBSERVING SABBATH

I'd like to share briefly about the practice of Sabbath, setting aside a period of time to cease from our daily routines, and receive our Lord's grace gift of rest.. This is one of the ten commandments, "Remember the Sabbath day by keeping it holy" (Ex. 20:8). Setting aside a full day to embrace a resting of one's body, mind and soul was a "covenant" that distinctly marked God's people as different from the pagan nations around them (Ex 31:12-17). Even today as we observe Sabbath we are reminded that we are citizens of another kingdom, with distinctive values.

In Genesis, it is clear that Creator-God built into the very fabric of creation a rhythm of rest. After six days of creative activity, the Lord Himself took rest! He created us in His image. He worked, then rested. So when we rest, we honor the way He made us. There are two core meanings of the word *"Shabbat."* One, to cease from striving, *to stop.* Also, *to celebrate.* It's amazing to me that no other Near Eastern civilization or religion has any notion of a god who takes rest or commands its adherents to take rest!

Yahweh commands His people Israel to set apart a day to cease from the stress of the activities and duties of daily life to just be together with Him and their loved ones. Sabbath was clearly a line in the sand marking a commitment to break from the cultural addictions of activity, accomplishment, and accumulation. *Sabbath is an opportunity to remind ourselves of who we really are. It is also an act of trust that as we rest, He takes care of our work and world without us!*

Let's be honest. Doing life in our everyday worlds has two major distractions—

*   External: constant digital data, entertainment, politics, busyness, personal obsessions, etc.

*   Internal: unceasing flow of our thoughts, emotions, desires, burdens

As modern day followers of Jesus, when we build Sabbath into our week, we are intentionally slowing our pace, and embracing the grace of rest (do what refreshes you!). We delight in the goodness of the Lord through reflective reading, prayers of gratitude and thanksgiving, worship, and time with family and friends, and good food! *Let me be clear—Sabbath is not just a "day off," but rather an opportunity to take a soul rest,* reminding ourselves of what really matters. It is a choice to mark out and protect a period of time to simply be God's chosen child and enjoy Him. In short, *to be reminded that my value is defined not by what I do, but by who I am.*

As challenging as it is to build a day like this into your schedule, I encourage you to begin taking steps towards observing Sabbath. In the busyness of our culture, this can look and feel like a "high bar"! Start simple, make small beginnings. Consider starting with an evening, or an 8- or 12-hour period that fits with the flow of your household or family. A few "starters" to consider:

- Get your house cleaned and in order the day before your Sabbath, so you can actually rest.

- Light a candle and welcome God's grace gift of rest. We always begin this way.

- Read and reflect briefly on a portion of Scripture.

- As hard as it is, put aside all cyber devices, homework, or anything work-related. Some families put all cyber devices in a box or container until Sabbath is over!

- Plan a simple, candle-lit meal, with unhurried conversation.

- Enjoy a favorite family game or activity.

- Spend time in nature or connecting with friends.

- Have a household or family time of worship and prayer.

- Take naps, or encourage everyone, "Do what refreshes you!"

Success is simply being intentional making space to welcome the grace of rest into your hearts and home. Don't get discouraged. Lapses will happen. Get past your guilt and begin again.

In our family, when our kids were in elementary school, we began experimenting with a Christian version of a Jewish Shabbat meal, lingering at the table for unhurried conversation, followed by family worship, a favorite family game and a special dessert.

When our son Josh was in grad school, we visited him in Philadelphia. Tom and I were so blessed to have him host us for his unique version of Sabbath, with candles providing the only light in his apartment, a special meal, and leading us in worship. He continues doing Sabbath with his family today, as they live fast-paced lives. He says, "We cannot live a healthy, balanced life without Shabbat, our day of rest."

Observing Sabbath is one of the classic spiritual disciplines. I commend you to take steps towards building this into the flow of your life, as a single, a household, or family. As you honor the Lord by observing the rhythm of Sabbath, pausing to take delight in Him, watch for and notice signs of His taking delight in you…refreshment, peace, joy.

My soul finds rest in God alone.

—Psalm 62:1

SPIRITUAL DISCIPLINES

The apostle Paul writes in Philippians 3, "Oh that I may know Him." That is, not just to know *about* the Lord, but to know Him *experientially.* Spiritual disciplines (sabbath, meditation, prayer, silence, solitude, and others) are essential in the process of knowing Jesus more intimately and growing deeper in our walk with Him.

We've all driven at night and benefitted from the guardrails on the side of the road which reflect the headlights to keep your car centered. *Spiritual disciplines serve as guardrails of the heart that bring me back to my center, which is purity and simplicity of devotion to Christ.* They guard my mind and will from wandering from the path, taking my own way. They reflect the image of Christ, He whom I want to know and become like.

As we explore the value and practice of the spiritual disciplines, I encourage you to keep the picture below in mind:

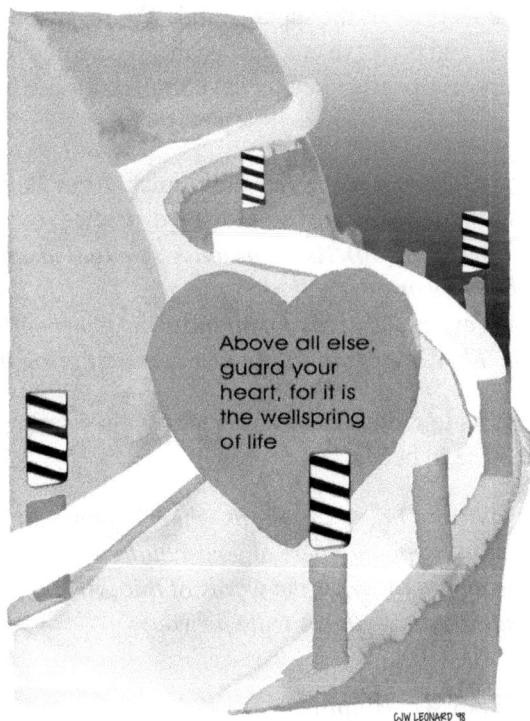

Above all else, guard your heart, for it is the wellspring of life

CJW LEONARD '98

PRACTICING SPIRITUAL DISCIPLINES

Holy habits that help me grow closer to God

My son, pay attention to what I say; listen closely to my words.
Do not let them out of your sight, keep them within your heart.
For they are life to those who find them and health to a man's whole body.
Above all else, guard your heart,
for it is the wellspring of life.

—Proverbs 4:20-23

The Hebrew word for "guard" has several meanings: to watch over, inspect, protect, keep, or preserve. In the noun form it means a confined place, a prison. Isn't it interesting to note that in the natural world our physical hearts are "guarded," "imprisoned" by our ribs? Often the Lord gives us a picture in the natural that reflects for us the supernatural. We are admonished above all else to watch over and preserve our spiritual heart, keeping it sensitive to Him. As we examine our hearts, they reveal our affections, what we value and choose to love.

Why this command? The Lord knows how quickly our hearts become hardened. He knows how easily we can become distracted, calloused, bent on our own ways (Isaiah 6:9,10*). As we practice spiritual disciplines, God uses them as tools that work the soil of our hearts. They do the "ground-breaking" work of getting the seed of truth into our heart-soil, preparing and nourishing it. They are essential for our spiritual growth.*

In his parting remarks to the Israelites, Moses brought a serious challenge that we would be wise to heed:

Set your minds and hearts on all the words which I command you
this day, that you may command them to your children,
that they may be watchful to do all the words of this law.
For it is not an empty and worthless trifle for you;
it is your very life.

—Deuteronomy 32:46, 47 (Amplified)

Keeping ourselves familiar with our Lord's commands and putting them into practice in the context of daily life is *not* about the doing of obligatory religious duties. It is *not* a drudge or a trifle! Learning to hear and heed God is *indeed our very life.*

As I give myself time to be silent before Him, listening, receiving and responding to Him, His truth begins to influence and change my choices. The character attributes of Jesus are actually formed within me. While this growth is a lifelong process, there are often specific points in time when He deals with areas of my inner life, transforming the patterns of my old life into His "image" (Spirit-controlled character). Paul describes this God-empowered process so beautifully in 2 Corinthians 3:17,18 when contrasting the old covenant with the new.

Now the Lord is the Spirit, and where the Spirit of the Lord is, there is freedom. And we all, who with unveiled faces contemplate the Lord's glory, are being transformed into his image with ever-increasing glory, which comes from the Lord, who is the Spirit.

My part is to be about beholding (contemplating) and pursuing God— seeing Him for who He is. **His part, through the work of His Spirit, is to be about molding me into the very likeness of His Son,** "with ever increasing glory" (an ongoing process.) We were created to receive from and respond to God. Why do we intentionally practice the spiritual disciplines? *To cultivate deeper relational intimacy and become like Christ.*

Our Work and God's Work

Let's define more clearly this difference between what we do, and what God does. Paul writes in Philippians 2:12: "Work out your own salvation [referring to spiritual growth that comes after we are justified in Christ] with fear and trembling, for God is at work in you to act according to his good purposes." There is a balance to be found between working out our salvation through the spiritual disciplines (our part) and God working it out within us (His part).

There is a vitally important secret of spiritual growth we need to understand. Because of Christ's atoning sacrifice, I am no longer under the pressure to try harder to become better. I cannot reform my own patterns of sin and selfishness. I cannot even resolve to "just be more like Jesus." *Through the cross, God has taken the initiative to put my old nature to death, and to implant within my humanity the seed and substance of a whole new life.* This seed nature itself stirs desire to seek and please the Lord. This new life, brought to me by the indwelling presence of the Holy Spirit, is the "new me," the "real me" who wants to cooperate in the process of being transformed into the very likeness of Jesus. Yes, I am responsible to build into my life regular disciplines of prayer, Bible reading, and service. But preceding these responses—even inspiring and empowering them—is a supernatural release of God's grace into my inner being. *He is not requiring me to live up to the standards of a holy life in my own strength.* That's just more religion. It's surely not freedom. No, we need to see that God has already created a "new me" inside, with a heart to become more like Jesus. If we can but realize this, revel in this amazing gift, and commit to "work out [our own] salvation," He Himself will release the power needed to do this. I encourage you to begin to notice these God-given desires that surface in you.

The practices I describe in this book are rightly called *disciplines* because they involve something we are responsible to do. But we must not fall into the bondage of legalism. That's just another prescription for frustration and failure. Neither should we do them with a hidden motive of manipulation, to somehow get what we want from God. If we practice the disciplines for the wrong reasons, they become a "form of godliness" with no real power to transform. No, instead, we practice these disciplines out of a newly implanted desire to be more like Jesus, and to position us to live a surrendered life. *This blessed new life is not attained by self- reformation. It is a gift of grace planted in the heart of every new believer. It is a work done in us, not by us!* As we respond to this gift, and cooperate in "working out" our continued growth, God Himself initiates and sustains the ongoing formation of Christ's life in us.

We must remember that the purpose of these disciplines is that they position us in a place where the Lord can do His work of grace within us as we yield to Him. They are the guardrails that guide our minds and emotions to be listening, responsive, and open to change.

Responding to God

How does this happen? One way the working out of my salvation occurs is through a daily practice of the disciplines that helps me receive from and respond to the Lord. Let me give you a picture of how this can look. I might feel convicted by the Scripture (Eph 4:29) that my speech has not been pleasing to God. First I agree with the Lord, confessing that this has been and still is a problem area. I get specific, asking Him to show me problems in my speech and whom I have wounded or offended by my words. I choose to be completely honest, repenting over the hurt and damage that my gossip, anger, and belittling of others has done. When I bring these things before God in honesty, and repent, He begins to bring forth in me the desire to change. Step by step He leads me. I begin to follow what He tells me to do. Through the work of the Holy Spirit, whom I have asked to give me strength and guidance, I repent to the people I have hurt, and I receive their forgiveness.

The next time the Spirit reveals to me that I have said something insensitive or hurtful, I recognize and choose to obey more readily. I practice a form of the discipline of abstinence, controlling my speech. The process of listening and responding begins to happen more quickly, more automatically. This is where the seed of truth has a transforming power and effect. *A changed life is always demonstrated by fruit.* In our daily relationships, in the busyness and stresses of life, and in our ordinary and mundane activities the Holy Spirit will nudge, prompt, even convict us if we are open-hearted toward Him.

We must also remember what a privilege it is to work out our own salvation. The Lord gives us a free will to **choose** to love Him, and through the spiritual disciplines we have the privilege and opportunity to express to our Lord this devotion. This must come out of sincere personal desire, not a stifling sense of obligation. When the disciplines are practiced with this attitude, our desire to continue in them grows.

Discipline as Training

The Apostle Paul also knew the value of the disciplines. In 1 Timothy 4:7 he writes, "Train yourself to be godly, for physical training is of some value, but godliness has value for all things." Training for godliness has value because it enables us to become like Jesus whom we love. Paul says, "Follow my example as I follow Christ." What was his example? In Philippians 3:8 he writes, "I consider everything a loss compared to the surpassing greatness of knowing Christ." All is considered loss compared to being in relationship with Jesus.

Paul explains this further in his Epistles: "Put off the old self, put on the new... submit your members as instruments of righteousness... submit your body as a living sacrifice... train your natural desires for godliness." *What would make any of us want to do that?* For me, the only reason would be my commitment and desire to know the Lord, and to become increasingly like Him. Do you hear what Paul is saying? *The Lord requires it of you.* It will cost you something, but in the end it is the only way to "train yourself to be godly."

Dealing with Resistance

We notice in ourselves—all of us— that there are times when we neglect or resist engaging in the spiritual disciplines. We exert effort and see too little change. There are times when we do not pursue Him because of our fears, disappointments, and discouragements. There are days we do not "feel" like reading the Word. We get distracted or put it off and then come to the end of the day without having spent any time with Him. Humanly, we have our ups and downs. But if we are seriously interested in growing spiritually, there needs to be a commitment to build spiritual practices into our lives.

Sometimes there are even deeper underlying reasons why we are resistant to these disciplines. Sometimes we come with a marred concept of who God really is, and how He relates to us. It affects how we think about Him and respond to Him. We may believe that God is one who could not truly love us, is tired of our failures, uninterested and distant from the important details of our lives. Or perhaps we see Him as one whom we can never please and who does not truly understand our struggles. Our faulty beliefs and the enemy's lies we listen to lead us to feelings of guilt, failure, and anger.

When we find ourselves with such a distorted view of God, we must stop and get honest with ourselves and ask the Lord. At what point did we withdraw, and why? We must also ask the Lord to reveal the real reasons for our resistances to practicing the disciplines, for these practices serve as the very guardrails that protect us, keep us in communion with Him, and guide us in discerning the voice of truth from lies.

For some, these resistances are more deeply rooted. I'd like to address a painful reality that many struggle with. Clearly, our Lord's desire and design is that His unconditional love is imprinted on and imparted into children and young adults. For those who have grown up in a healthy family system, hearing such phrases as "You are the Lord's beloved," or "the Lord delights in you," they have capacity to believe and receive the blessing of authentic love, anchored in the emotional security of their family of origin and/or a Church community. But for many, this unconditional love of a Creator-God is short-circuited, distorted, or absent altogether. This leaves a vulnerable soul with a very fragile self-image, and a pressure to perform to earn affirmation and value. This can trace to emotional and physical abuse. But a soul can also be damaged by negligence, an absence of affirmation and blessing. In either case, across this spectrum, a wounded soul wrestles with a painful, core question: "Am I *really* loveable just for who I am, not for what I do or how I perform?"

To be emotionally healthy, a growing soul needs to see, hear and feel the security of a love that affirms and protects. In short, emotional safety and security. When this love is experienced, it creates a dual capacity to both receive and rest in love, and to love others. But here's the painful truth. When this is short-circuited or distorted through a wounding of words or neglect, there are consequences. Generally, two things happen. There is emotional damage, leaving a "hole in the soul." And there are deeply submerged reactions of anger, unforgiveness, and mistrust. So, with people who process this kind of pain, we see this syndrome: bouncing back and forth from hurt (resisting and sabotaging authentic spiritual growth), and reaching out for healing (hoping for an encounter with real love).

Dear reader, if this is you, or a friend, spouse, or family member dealing with this kind of resistance, you probably feel "stuck," sometimes hopeless. I encourage you to seek out a caring friend, a pastor, mentor, professional counselor, or someone gifted in emotional healing ministry. Share your pain, confess your anger and unforgiveness, and pursue a path of healing. *The person and presence of the Holy Spirit, our "Counselor and Comforter," is always available to you!* He alone, working through healing vessels, can break through these submerged resistances to going forward and growing in Christlikeness. For further help dealing with these resistances, I highly recommend to you the ministry of Peter Scazzero, in particular his book *Emotionally Healthy Spirituality.*

The Joy of Obedience

In summary, here's the spirit of practicing spiritual disciplines. *It begins with desire, and then obedience motivated by love.* Cooperation with God's Spirit requires heart choices and discipline. *The choices we make reveal what we really believe about God!* And He continually brings us to "grace places" where our choices and obedience are truly joyful and not burdensome.

Our single pursuit is to know Jesus. And godliness, becoming like Christ, is the result of this pursuit. As we keep an eternal perspective, all will be considered loss compared to knowing Him! (Phil. 3:7-10) *As we practice the spiritual disciplines we find that they are the tools that plow up the hardened soil of our hearts.* As we more regularly encounter His character and love, our heart soil becomes ready for the planting of His seeds for growth and godliness.

The spiritual disciplines, practiced with a humble teachable heart . . .

... bring intimacy and growth in my relationship to God.

... bring revelation of God's character to me.

... create a place and a time to be with the one I love.

... are the guardrails of the heart that bring me back to the center, which is purity and simplicity of devotion to Christ.

... enable me to behold Him; to gaze upon Him whom I love.

... mold and shape my choices to be godly, so Christ's character is manifest in me and I am conformed to His image.

... are the guardrails of the heart that keep me listening to and receiving the truth.

... build holy habits that bring maturity to my growth.

... give me the privilege and opportunity to express to my Lord my devotion and love for Him.

... position me so that the Lord can do his work of grace within me as I yield to Him.

... keep me from being squeezed into the world's mold. Instead, I am molded and shaped by the Word of God and His Spirit.

... are essential to my relationship with God.

Taking Time to Reflect

1. Think about your own motivation for practicing the disciplines. Do you do them out of duty (expectation, obligation, performance), or out of a desire to cultivate a deeper relationship with God?

2. Reflect back on the section talking about resistances. Which, if any, do you identify with? Bring these to the Lord in prayer. Consider also sharing them with your spouse or a trusted friend for prayer and accountability. Make a resolve to face and deal with issues that would hinder your ability to grow spiritually.

3. Could your spiritual growth be hindered by distorted concepts of God? Take a few moments to reflect on your family history. Are there people in your life that wounded you? If so, to what extent have you resolved your hurt and reactive anger? Make an effort to get to the *root* of any unresolved mistrust, bitterness, or anger. Reflect also on your spiritual history. Pinpoint disappointments or disillusionment you have experienced in your walk that have caused you to distance yourself from the Lord. If your understanding of God is distorted, or your ability to entrust your life to Him hindered, you may struggle practicing the disciplines. Perhaps it would be helpful for you to slowly read through the gospel of John, only noticing who Jesus *really* is, and not perhaps who you might think He is.

4. What concrete steps might you take to advance in your personal training in godliness? (e.g., spending intentional time alone with God, seeking out a mentor, submitting to the accountability of a small group, memorizing Scripture).

5. As you make renewed efforts at putting these disciplines increasingly into practice, ask Him to make them a joyful obedience, and not burdensome.

SOLITUDE

Jesus often withdrew to lonely places and prayed.

—Luke 5:16

One of those days Jesus went out to a mountainside to pray, and spent the night praying to God.

—Luke 6:12

Often, I think, when we see the word "solitude," we picture a monk in a cave, withdrawn from all normal social interaction, or a spiritually-minded person confined behind cloistered walls. While most of us never have or never will live a monastic life, we can learn much from their commitment to seek times and seasons of solitude, and to minimize life's ceaseless distractions. For Christians serious about spiritual growth, solitude, for any length of time, is a discipline that opens a door for God to release a greater measure of His Son's life *into* us, and to work *out* of us the sin and self-centeredness bound up in our old nature.

In solitude, I make space for uninterrupted time in a place free of my typical life distractions. My aim is to be truly alone with God. Solitude is about being set free from the constancy of doing and evaluating my life in reference to others. *Most importantly, in this set-apart time, we make space, in David's words from Psalm 27, to simply behold the Lord, to gaze upon His beauty and to worship Him.* I am also able to enter into practicing other spiritual disciplines.

Also in solitude, God has opportunity to awaken deep things within us. Solitude helps us sort out our heart distractions and renews and re-centers our true desire to seek Him. Solitude can bring us into a place of spiritual rest. When we truly encounter His accepting presence, we are able to cease from our strivings, and just *be* with Him.

Let's begin with a word of instruction from Jesus:

When you pray, go into your room, close the door and pray to your Father, who is unseen. Then your Father, who sees what is done in secret, will reward you.

—Matthew 6:6

For years now, as I have stilled my heart before the Lord, He has continually brought this Scripture to me. Oh, how I love this prayer closet, the inner sanctuary of the heart where Jesus dwells and where I can abide and hear His Word to me! The Lord instructs me when I pray to *shut the door*. It is a place where there are no external distractions, a place where I release pre-occupations and center my heart and mind on Him alone.

Centering on His presence in this way is a spiritual discipline. I find that I am drawn to this closet for varied reasons. Sometimes I come through simple, loving obedience. Other times there is a deep and intentional desire to simply draw near to God, or I come when I am burdened or bothered, and I need to pour out my heart to the Lord. *The important thing is to just come.*

In my journey, sitting in silence first felt a bit uncomfortable. Or, it felt like "nothing was happening." But silence often exposes how much I get stuck in my own head, reinforced by familiar voices, distractions and activities (or even productivities!). Sometimes it's hard to slow down and break out of this mindset. Thus, my prayer, "Lord, help me now to be still, and listen." I continually need to remind my soul to settle down...*there is no place to go right now...nothing else more important to do.* " Just be with Him.

*Solitude is not just being alone. It is time intentionally given, in a protected place, to be alone with God. I would describe it as **purposeful aloneness.*** During such times, I choose to put distance between myself and all that constantly demands my time, attention and energy. I give God's Spirit opportunity to break the compulsive habits that invade my life from the surrounding culture (watching TV, keeping up with social media, texting, shopping, phoning, e-mailing, or tending to the demands of my job). Understand that when you start into solitude, you will need to quiet both outward and inward "noise" and distractions. It will take time for your rambling thoughts to be stilled, your emotions to settle, and the press of circumstances and decisions to fade to the edges. This is normal.

Even though I shut out the external distractions, there are certainly internal ones! Every time I have decided to sit and wait on God, the restlessness of my humanity is quickly exposed. My mind meanders (or even scatters!) in every direction; my emotions are driven by my moods; my will is distracted by what it wants. Distractions bubble up to the surface. As they do, I begin to release them one by one in prayer. Often, I write these down on my "offload list" and then simply *return to centering on the Lord.* You may have to return several times in prayer and say, "Lord, I am here." This sometimes is a continual process. If the distraction persists then I need to honestly look within to see what the issue really is. Distractions can reveal what in our hearts needs to be more deeply processed with God. Ask the Lord, "what do you want me to know?" Am I indulging in worry? Is there a strained relationship I need to give attention to? Identify what's bothering you. *Spending purposeful alone time in solitude will change your life and relationship with the Lord. Wouldn't you like to live your life out of a reservoir of internal strength, a connectedness to God, rather than reacting to life's circumstances and challenges in the energy of your soul?*

We would be wise to heed this counsel from A. W. Tozer, a companion of Jesus who has been a spiritual guide to many:

> *Retire from the world each day to some private spot.*
> *Stay in the secret place till the surrounding noises*
> *begin to fade out of your heart,*
> *and a sense of God's presence envelops you…*
> *Listen for the inward voice till you learn to recognize it.*

I know I'll never find deep communion with God searching for Him only with my mind. I cannot, by an act of will, demand or expect Him to reveal Himself to me. *I believe the intensity of my heart's desire to know Him more deeply and love Him more fully opens a door to intimacy. In a positive sense, I would describe this as a "holy heartache."* I have found that solitude is where this kind of desire for God is best cultivated. It is here that I discover my deepest joy—I am known and fully loved.

Silence is a vital part of solitude. I am more quick to listen than to speak. I don't just refrain from talking. No, I cultivate a humble, teachable, receptive posture of listening, wanting to hear the "still, small voice" of God's Spirit. *My conversation is not a monologue. It is "prayerful listening."* In silence, I empty myself of my words, releasing my control of the conversation, so I am not just listening to my own thoughts and opinions. I am *making space* to actually listen to the Spirit actively speaking to me, such as through a specific Scripture, the words of a song, a thought highlighted to me, or a prompting.

Silence also gives me an increasing awareness of His presence. It works to bring my words into submission, and allows the power of the pure Word of the Lord to come to me. Silence is a core component of solitude.

Learning to be silent in His presence is simply not natural, but rather a supernatural way of listening. We're so accustomed to endless noise, things going on in our daily lives and culture-- the perpetual pings of a text or Instagram, or dings from WhatsApp, that we find we are uncomfortable with silence.

Let's be honest here. Do you ever find yourself discouraged by or even dreading silence? Maybe you have thoughts like these: "This seems like just me again, same old thoughts. I feel stuck. I'm just not very good at hearing God's voice. I guess something's wrong with me. Maybe I'm not spiritual enough for this."

If you struggle with this kind of self-talk, I suggest you begin with Jesus' promised gift of the Holy Spirit, and remind yourself of the truth that He is not merely just *available to you,* but rather *abiding in you,* desiring to speak to you. Jesus was clear, "My sheep hear My voice, and follow Me." *But there's another voice, that of the enemy, a liar and accuser who agrees with and aggravates your negative self-talk. When engaging silence, it is very important to recognize and renounce his lies.*

A true "conversation" involves two-way communication. When you and I make space in silence to be more intentional listening, we can learn how the Holy Spirit speaks to us. As you settle into silence, simply be restfully present. Do your best to quiet your thoughts, beginning perhaps with Samuel's prayer, "Speak, Lord, your servant longs to hear Your voice." Then just notice what is surfacing in you. This could sound like a gentle whisper, an impression that rises in you, a specific thought, a word, an image, a song, perhaps a noticeable sense of His nearness and love. Sit a moment, unrushed. Simply just notice what you're becoming aware of. It may be clear, or raise this question: "Lord, is this really You…or me?" Then make a space of silence to notice what He is bringing to you. This is your way of listening as He speaks.

Cultivate an attitude of attentive listening. Develop your own way of conversing with the Lord in an interactive way. The Spirit uses these quiet spaces we make to speak to us. Of course there is a lifelong learning curve here. The more you make space to be still and listen, you will come to realize

He *is* speaking and you *are* hearing His voice more than you even realized!

You might start this practice for just a few minutes each time, settling your mind and quieting your soul, simply waiting, watching, noticing and responding. Increase the time as you are comfortable and desirous. Don't feel pressure to make anything happen. Remember, even Elijah had a challenge learning how to hear God's voice! He did not hear the holy One speaking in the wind, the earthquake or the fire. No, he heard the Lord through a "still, small voice." Samuel had his own learning curve, beginning as a boy, learning to discern the gentle voice of God from human voices.

You're a learner. Be patient with yourself, and know that the Lord in you is pleased that you're even coming and longing to hear His voice. *Making space for silence in solitude is vitally important. It trains our spiritual ears to be more intentional in our listening and more attentive in our hearing.* In this journey of learning to hear His voice, you might find it helpful and encouraging to journal your encounters with Him.

So why don't we seek this solitude more often? I believe there are times when we feel apprehensive about our "alone time" with God. In the absence of all the normal recognition and approval from others in my daily life, I come face to face with who I really am in the depths of my being.

This can be the hardest part of solitude: facing and seeing my shadow side, who I really am. Being alone with God is like looking carefully in a mirror, and seeing what's really there (like wrinkles and blemishes). I come to see my secret sins, unaccepting attitudes towards others, motives, control issues, fears, worries, prejudices. This can be troubling. Sometimes I just don't want to see or acknowledge the real me! Sometimes my faulty "God view" makes me fear He is only waiting to correct me, will be disappointed, or turn His face from me. Solitude provides a space and time where I can expose these parts of me to a merciful, understanding Lord who sees and is not surprised by who I am, and is there to help and support me like a good parent.

One day as I read Psalm 139, the first and last verses alone stood out and impacted me. *"O Lord, you have searched me and know me. You know when I sit, when I rise; you perceive my thoughts from afar."* This brought a kind of comfort to me, because I know that God already sees and knows every tiny detail about me. I'm always in His presence, known and seen. I meditated on this for some time, and even though it made me feel vulnerable and disappointed in what I saw in myself, it also strengthened my knowledge that I am secure in His love. Soaking in this truth has anchored me more deeply in Him and removed my resistances to being vulnerable. There's nothing hidden.

I then read verses 23-24, "Search me O God, and know my heart: test me, and know my thoughts. See if there is any wicked way in me and lead me in the way everlasting." I saw this as an invitation to experience being loved by Him, even in the dark places of my soul. I began to realize *that God is a "safe examiner."* I bring everything into the light of His presence. This awareness and willingness to surrender my thoughts and emotions, places where I feel "stuck" or struggle with secret sins or failures, is where I truly experience the embrace of God's unconditional love. And He knows how to personally *lead* me.

In solitude, the Lord invites me into what I choose to call "processing prayer." We could also call this a "pouring out" of one's heart, positive or negative. Sometimes I find myself struggling with what He has shown me. For me, "processing prayer" is then that personal communication between me and my Lord that seeks to bridge the gap between what I currently am, and what God is wanting to make me. It is the giving of my true self to Him. Jacob (his given name means striver, usurper) wrestled with God for a prolonged time at the Jabbok river (Gen. 32:22-32). When God prevailed and won the battle by breaking Jacob's hip, He blessed his servant and changed his name to Israel ("he struggles with God"). *He was permanently changed.* Often, like Jacob, our alone times are marked by an honest acknowledgement of who we really are, and purposeful wrestling. And this is an authentic wrestling. I can choose to let Him break and shape me, or back away in fear or unbelief, postponing His dealings with me until another time. But in times of solitude, as we struggle like Jacob, we encounter the One who knows our name and makes His grace available to us, transforming us by His Spirit.

Looking at God's dealings with Jacob, keep this truth ever-present in your mind—*He wants me to be who I am meant to be, a unique "one-of-a-kind" soul, an identity shaped in His image.*

So, here are some of my initial simple steps for engaging "processing prayer," when I struggle:

- "Lord, help me discern and renounce any lies and accusations from the evil one."

- "Lord, what do you want me to see and know about what I have opened up to you?"

- I identify and name it: envy, discontent, resistant attitudes.

- I go deeper, "Lord, what is the root of this? Why did I react this way?"

- I follow through with what seems to be the next step He is inviting me into.

- I give myself grace!

So, solitude is a "purposeful aloneness" that can produce profound spiritual growth. In time, I learn the freedom to be who I really am. When I realize that I can't really hide anyway, I have liberty to pour out my deepest emotions, unveil my struggles, confess my sins, and give God opportunity to speak into my life, even to "break my hip!" Most of these times are personal struggles that we keep hidden from others. As part of our pilgrimage, God exposes the patterns of sin and self-centeredness that are un-Christlike and releases the power of His Spirit to transform these patterns into the character of Jesus.

Let me be clear about the role of prayer in times of solitude. I can and do pray apart from my alone times with the Lord. But deep heart attentiveness and spiritual renewal occur most in my life during these set-aside times of solitude. Without them, I find my prayers are focused more on the here-and-now issues of daily life. I am not as in touch with my deeper thoughts and feelings. In solitude I come face-to-face with my brokenness and sin. Prayer becomes an offering to God, a releasing of these areas of need, and a receiving of His forgiveness and healing grace.

How often do you say to yourself, "Lord, I just wish I could have more to offer in helping others along in their spiritual journeys?" This is a normal motivation of a mature, growing believer. Here's an encouraging truth. The more that my old self decreases and the power of Christ increases, my spiritual sensitivity to others also increases. There is a newfound strength to speak and minister to the pain of others that flows from an inner reservoir of grace that the Father has poured into me. This is one of the outcomes of solitude—we freely give that which we have received.

How often, and for how long do we practice solitude? This will of course be different for everyone. There are seasons and circumstances of life when making and taking time to be alone with God will look different. When my children were infants, when I finally found a time and space for solitude, I fell dead asleep! Honestly, I never felt judged by the Lord. He knew my spirit was willing, but my flesh was weak! So I began to plan for Tom to watch the kids on Saturday morning, so I could have some extended time for meditation, journaling, and personal prayer. During the rest of my week, I would find available time and space for solitude in a day to meditate on what the Lord had spoken to me in my extended time. Whatever it looks like in your season of life, just be intentional about regularly building in times of solitude.

You could also consider scheduling in a half-day or a day away for alone time. Plan ahead and set aside some short devotional readings to stir your heart. Learn to offer the Lord your own expression of personal worship and adoration in song and prayer. You might also think about taking an overnight one or two times a year at a retreat center. Your longing for purposeful aloneness will likely increase, as will the depth and meaning of your personal appointments with Him.

Life has its endless ebbs and flows, and can be very demanding in certain seasons. In His humanity, Jesus had to deal with these demands. Scripture reveals that Jesus often sought *intentional* times of solitude to be alone with the Father. I personally think His highest priority in those times was to *withdraw from* the demands and pressures of his public life, and simply *draw near to* His Father. No agenda, just a son enjoying the blessing of being with his Father!

While we commit to take such times to seek God's presence in solitude, we must not come under a legalistic bondage of guilt and failure if we miss the mark. Remember always, God is *for* us. He understands our frames and frailties. Taking time for solitude and silence will add a new depth and dimension to your journey with Jesus and empower you as you serve others. I encourage you to make some simple beginnings. Building solitude into our busy lives is a highly intentional discipline that provides the context for a more regular and effective practice of the other spiritual disciplines.

Draw apart from the outward frenzy and draw near to God. Learn to practice the seeking of His Presence in the secret, quiet place, and your inner life will never be the same.

Consider also the treasures you can receive in solitude. In David's words, "The Lord confides in those who fear Him" (Ps 25:14). He shares personal revelation, wisdom, next steps, vision, comfort, songs, specific timely words, and other insights. I begin to learn to recognize His voice to me. There is so much I miss if I do not spend time in solitude with Him. What a privilege that my Lord would confide what is on His heart with me, and for me! In solitude as I sit in the light of His loving presence, there is the freedom of the "real me" to be exposed, and I begin to recognize hindrances to becoming like Him. I bring my "just as I am" to Him. The truth is, each encounter with the Lord in solitude is entirely different in every way, and should be filled with anticipation because you are meeting the God who made you and is *for you.*

Hearing God in Solitude: A Personal Story

My husband and I have raised our family in our home for 34 years now. About ten years ago I was in the upstairs bathroom, routinely opening the small window-blinds. As I had numerous times, I noticed the beautiful field and view adjacent to our property, with a forest at its edge. In that moment, a new idea came to me. I went down the hallway to my office that I have used for 24 years, and a light went on inside of me! What if we put a window in this office? I would always have a beautiful view of this open field and the forest.

Why hadn't I seen this before? I ran downstairs, asked my husband to come up. I excitedly explained what had come to me, and why we needed a window! He kindly agreed, but we were not sure it was structurally possible. We called a contractor friend. He informed us it could be done, and to our delight and total surprise, he insisted that he wanted to do this as a gift for us! We were so deeply touched that he would use his skills to bless us! This was beyond what we could have envisioned.

So the day came when I got the 6 x 5 window. I sat in my special "prayer chair," which for decades had been my sanctuary and place of solitude to be with the Lord. I have worshipped, prayed, processed, and lived through my "book of psalms" in my life as I have poured out my heart in this secret place.

As I sat, I was so overwhelmed by all the light coming into the room! It felt "right," like it should have been there all along. I soaked in the beauty of the puffy clouds, the open field, and the deer running along the edge of the forest. I couldn't move. I just remained still…then tears began to flow. Tears of overwhelming gratitude and joy with this new vision before me, but also mixed with some regret. I realized in that moment that for 24 years I had been sitting, looking at a wall, missing sunrises, sunsets, light in the room, deer running through the field, sheep on the hill, and changing seasons!! It took all that time to see right in front of me that which was always possible. I had missed so much not having a window!

Even as my cup overflowed with gratitude, and I soaked in the light streaming into the room, I poured out my mixed "prayer tears" to Him. I realized I was receiving the gift of a window purposed to bring me light and sight and enjoyment because He wanted to give me this gift to bless me for years to come. What a difference this made in my room!

Then the Lord's still small voice spoke to me: *"Terri…You have some walls in your soul where I also have wanted to put windows."* Those words really surprised me and caused me to pause…and listen. I didn't feel I was being corrected, but rather invited to receive something more than just a physical blessing.

I could feel a curiosity, more like a joy, surface in me as I was experiencing what a gift a window can be! *What might that mean for my soul?* It almost felt like He waited until this moment to speak these words to me.

In the next few days, as I sat in solitude, I asked Him, "What are those walls right now?" One thing that came to me was feeling inadequate in certain situations, "I don't have what it takes to do this!" I noticed ways this was holding me back from taking some life-changing steps of trust. I continued in prayer, processing with the Lord some lies I had believed and root reasons for my inadequacies. He gently led me into some new revelation, and some small, simple next steps. The wall was being removed.

I realized that day, when my ears heard and my eyes were open, the walls in my office room were breached, and a blessing was gained. I responded by asking the Lord to do the same with the walls in my life that were getting in the way of me receiving all He had in mind for me. Sometimes it's messy work, and I struggle, but I have now grown to welcome His windows.

As I look back to that day, I realized I was just doing an ordinary daily thing… opening up a blind! He gave me a blessed idea, and then provided in surprising ways how we could receive His love gift to us. It could have just remained an enjoyable gift from Him. A window with a great view! But…it was in solitude, as I made time to sit with Him that his real "soul gift "was given to me. *He used the "ordinary" to get my attention, then He did the "extraordinary!"* This experience has also brought awareness to me to notice and be attentive to those times He has something for me to learn or know through the "ordinary" circumstances of life. I reflect on that in solitude.

Through the years, as I have sat in my chair looking out my window, I'm still overcome with gratitude. I often think what I would have missed and not heard if I had not made space to be with Him. So much light and delight and healing has come into my soul since that day!

As I have said before…sometimes in solitude His voice seems clear or as loud as thunder, but other times we are just quietly reminded of who He is and His love for us. We are to remain open to receive whatever He gives, and to rest in that truth that the real purpose is to *be* with Him.

Taking Time to Reflect

1. Take a few minutes to reflect over the past two weeks of your life. Can you recall a "niche" of time when you were not working a task, solving a problem, watching TV, reading or pursuing a hobby, but instead intentionally quiet, alone and seeking the Lord? If you have not had times like this, you might ask yourself why not? Take some time to process in prayer any specific resistances to solitude that you discern.

2. Get out your calendar and mark out some times for solitude in the week ahead, with lengths of time that work for you. Decide also on a place. Whatever you choose, write it on your calendar now. If you've already been experiencing some regular times of solitude in your walk, you may want to schedule in a half day retreat, perhaps even a day away.

3. If you have not practiced being silent in His presence, simply start with one minute of silence. Take a deep breath to still your soul. Say, "Lord,

I am here." Or "Lord, my eyes are on you." Then just sit in silence for a minute. If distracting thoughts come, then repeat, "Lord, I am here." If necessary, continue to re-center using this phrase with each distracting thought. You will notice that soon you'll be able to increase your times of silence and begin to learn to hear His voice in new ways.

4. If you have not built silence into your times of solitude, you can begin by praying through a short Scripture (Matt. 11:28-30, "Come to me, learn from me, I am gentle in heart"). Read it, be silent, listen, and notice what surfaces in you. Take another minute in silence. Continue in this way, reading and listening, taking note of what you are hearing.

BIBLICAL MEDITATION
An Overview: Soaking in Scriptural Truth

When I think of scriptural meditation, the word picture that comes to my mind is that of putting a *soaker hose* on the soil of my heart. In meditation, I remain focused on one portion of Scripture, soaking in it day and night for a season, until the Lord works the verse into my heart, and it becomes internalized and personalized. ***Meditation is the irrigation system of our souls!***

Psalm 1 describes this practice:

Blessed is the man who does not walk in the counsel of the wicked
or stand in the way of sinners or sit in the seat of mockers.
But his delight is in the law of the Lord,
and on his law he meditates day and night.
He is like a tree planted by streams of water,
which yields its fruit in season and whose leaf does not wither.
Whatever he does prospers.

Deuteronomy 6:4-9 gives us a practical picture of the impact of God's truth on everyday living.

Hear O Israel: The Lord our God, the Lord is one.
Love the Lord your God with all your heart and with all your soul
and with all your strength. These commandments that I give you today
are to be upon your hearts. Impress them on your children.
Talk about them when you sit at home and when you walk along the road,
when you lie down and when you get up. Tie them as symbols on your
hands and bind them on your foreheads. Write them on the doorframes of
your houses and on your gates.

Clearly, God calls those who follow Him to soak in and saturate themselves with truth, live it out in the flow of everyday life, and impart it to others. True meditation is a lifestyle! Also, as we meditate day and night, we behold Him and our hearts become sanctuaries of worship.

The practice of "meditation" entails a personal encounter with the living

Word of God. Moses instructed his successor Joshua to engage this practice (Josh 1:7, 8). There are two words for "meditation" in Hebrew: "Haga," speaking Scripture repetitively in a low, soft voice, sort of like murmuring. "Sichah" carries the meaning of musing over and contemplating specific content. *Thus, we can say that meditation is a repetitive recitation of and reflection on Scriptural truth, useful for soaking in passages both small and large.* I may also choose to meditate on a particular theme or focus, such as an attribute of God, or walking in the fruits of the Spirit. In meditation, I may also cross-reference with other passages of Scripture. I may ask, what does this passage say or mean?

In the course of Church history, there arose a *defined approach* to meditation that centers primarily on one's relationship with the Lord, and personal, transformative encounter with God's Word. Saint Bernard in the 6th century was one of the first to utilize this approach. He named it "lectio divina," divine reading. In the 12th century, an Italian monk named Guigo gave further clarity to steps for engaging lectio. Ignatius then later developed the practice we are familiar with to this day.

Later in the book I'll lay out the steps for engaging lectio divina. To be clear, lectio *is* meditation, but intended more for engaging Scripture in a *prayerful, soul-listening way*, a personal encounter with a specific, single portion of the Word. One does not look for themes or cross-references.

In this section, I'd like to share some thoughts on the value and practice of meditation.

What Meditation Is

Meditation is... feeding on the Word of God, by pondering and reviewing thoughts until I absorb them into my mind and heart.

Meditation is... taking a good long look at Scripture — not glancing at it, but gazing steadily into its precepts; not reading and leaving, but reading and cleaving.

Meditation is... listening, and allowing the Holy Spirit to apply the Word to my heart so that the Word becomes personalized and internalized.

Meditation is... a means by which God reveals Himself to me and speaks to me personally through His Word.

Meditation is... a discipline that cultivates in me a listening heart.

Meditation is... the Lord using a passage to do "ground breaking" in my life. He works the truth of the verse into the soil of my life as I surrender to Him.

Meditation is... more than reading — it is prayer, communicating with the Lord. It is sitting down with my friend, the Lord, and letting Him speak to me. As I listen, and as He speaks, I allow His thoughts to "sink in," and I respond to Him.

Why Meditate?

As one seeking to know and obey the Lord ...

- I am reminded of who God is.

- I bring the little "i am" of my life into the Presence of the "Great I AM."

- I am affirmed in my true identity as a beloved child of God.

- I still my soul and draw into intimacy with the Lord.

- I believe that His truth will renew my mind.

- I find rest for my soul in the midst of life's stress.

- I receive revelation from the Holy Spirit that calls and empowers me to change and grow.

Several years ago I spent a season of time in Proverbs 4:20-27. It begins, "My son (daughter!) pay attention to what I say; listen closely to my words." The immediate picture that came to mind was a flashback of when my children were small. At times when they were distracted, I would take my hands, cup them around their small cheeks, look them straight in the eye and say, "Pay attention...look at my eyes...you need to listen." I would keep my hands positioned there, while I quietly gave them instruction. Believe me, their little flushed faces were wide-eyed and listening!

This is what happens to me as I meditate on Scripture in my own life. While doing the ordinary tasks of life the Lord stops me in my distracted, wayward moments (of which there are many), by quickening that portion of the Word to my mind. It is like He has turned me towards Him and He is holding my little face in His loving hands, looking deeply into my eyes, speaking clear and timely words to me. In those few moments, He has my *undivided attention.* My heart is re-routed, and I follow His instruction.

When to Meditate

As we have seen, in Joshua 1:8, 9 and Psalm 1:2, we find exhortations to meditate continually, "day and night." This should be my aim as I seek to walk moment-by-moment in the light of truth. But one can also mark out special moments, places, and circumstances in which to meet the Lord in His Word, wait on Him and receive revelation. Give God the best time of your day.

Oh how I love your law! I meditate on it all day long...
How sweet are your words to my taste,
Sweeter than honey to my mouth.

—Psalm 119:97, 103

BIBLICAL MEDITATION
Going Deeper: Revelation to Transformation

In our overview of meditation in the last section, I quoted Psalm 1:1-3 from the NIV. I'd like us to look at this passage again, from the Amplified Bible.

Blessed is the man...whose delight and desire are in the law of the Lord, and on His law—the precepts, the instructions, the teachings of God— he habitually meditates (ponders and studies) by day and by night. And he shall be like a tree firmly planted (and tended) by the streams of water, ready to bring forth his fruit in season, his leaf also shall not fade or wither, and everything he does shall prosper (and come to maturity).
—Psalm 1:1-3 (Amplified)

It is no coincidence that the very first Psalm depicts the servant of God who is truly blessed, and explains why. Spiritual fruitfulness is a direct result of soaking in truths that are eternal. This is not meant to be a drudgery. Neither does God intend this to be a religious duty. No, truth is to be the "delight and desire" of the lover of God. Further, it is clear that walking in truth is to be "24/7," a lifestyle. If I am resolved to absorb the principles of the Word, David assures me of four results: 1) I'll grow into a strong, spiritual tree, with deep roots drawing the freshest water, 2) fruit will appear "in season," 3) I won't wither away in times of drought (trials, tests, devotional dry times), and 4) I will taste of a God-produced prosperity. What an encouraging promise!

The question for you and me, living in the stress and press of this world is this: ***Do we really believe this conditional promise, and will we choose to build regular times of abiding in the Word of God into our busy lives?***

How easily and regularly our minds and moods are led astray: thoughts about our interests, what we should be doing; thoughts about other people, and what *they* should be doing; thoughts about what others think, feeling inadequate, wrestling with fears or anxieties; feeling sad or discouraged in response to circumstances. There are so many ways that our minds are held captive and led astray from the simplicity — the singleness of heart — of purity and devotion to Christ (See 2 Cor. 11:3).

How will meditation change my life? It cultivates in us a listening heart. Every day we are influenced by the voices and values of the world, our own flesh, and an accuser who knows our vulnerabilities all too well. These voices work to continually squeeze us into the patterns of our fallen world, leading us astray from living in the reality of His kingdom that we've been born into and belong to. So, how can we learn to know more consistently when God's Spirit is speaking, convicting, correcting, and guiding us? Paul's words are highly relevant here: *"Do not be conformed to this world—this age, fashioned after and adapted to its external, superficial customs. But be transformed (changed) by the (entire) renewal of your mind—by its new ideals and its new attitude." (Rom. 12:2a, Amplified).*

Webster defines renewal as making something new again by replacing what is old, re-establishing something to its original condition. Our mind is the object of this renewal. Taking time to meditate on truth gives the Holy Spirit direct access to our innermost thoughts. We give Him opportunity to break us free from worldly, cultural thinking, and to mold our minds to think according to the values of the spiritual kingdom. *God is interested in nothing less than a major renewal of both how and what we think!* And He made us with the capacity to renew our minds.

How are we renewed? When the Holy Spirit enters the life of a repentant sinner who has accepted Jesus' sacrifice for his sin, God begins a gradual re-creation of the "image" (nature) that humankind bore before the Fall. Our new nature—the infusion of the life of Christ by the Holy Spirit—begins to permeate our thinking, order our values, and give us power to change our old, self-centered ways. As "new creatures," we begin a process of transformation from the inside out. God's life within us gives strength to our "inner man" to increasingly order the thinking and actions of our "outer man." Empowered from within, we have the ability to choose to do all that He taught us to do. We are able to follow in His ways.

So, how do we experience this transformation? While there are many disciplines that contribute to spiritual growth, *I believe that learning to regularly meditate on biblical truth is the most effective thing we can do.* Whereas Eastern religions would tell us to empty our minds, becoming like Jesus is about filling our minds with the life-changing Word of God. We spend time soaking in it, reflecting on it, and allowing it to replace the thought patterns and lies that were a part of our old, unregenerate lives. *There is a vital point to understand here: God's truth is literally alive, endued with a supernatural power that changes those who take it in*. It is life for the soul. Here's how the writer of Hebrews describes it:

For the Word of God is alive and active. Sharper than any double-edged sword, it penetrates even to dividing soul and spirit, joints and marrow; it judges the thoughts and attitudes of the heart.

—Hebrews 4:12

We must take a long pause and let this Scripture speak to us. We read here that the Word is alive, powerful, penetrating and accurately discerning our deepest thoughts and motives. *So we can now see we do not want to engage in the Word in a casual or lighthearted way!* The seed of the Word needs to be planted in fertile soul soil. So we must come to it with a submitted heart, postured to listen, being teachable and receptive. We need to have a welcoming attitude that invites Him to probe and even pierce our souls, so He has freedom to examine, expose and speak. As we are available in this way, Jesus meets us *in* the Word, and the Holy Spirit works powerfully *through* the Word. As we do this, we remember that Jesus knows us, is gentle and humble in heart, and understands the frailties of our humanity. So we are safe to honestly say to Him, "My soul is…, or I trust you with…"

When we really grasp the potency of this truth, we'll be increasingly motivated to literally spend time in that *living* Word of God that penetrates and changes us from old to new, and from the inside out. This can only happen, however, as we truly believe in and act on the precepts of the Word as our very life. When God quickens our spirit by the impartation of His truth, then the thoughts of our minds, changeable emotions and the impulses of our bodies come under increased control of His Spirit. As we actively listen, we tune into, dwell on and receive God's thoughts, His ways and will. We begin to hear his personal voice speaking. *In time, my old way of thinking, feeling and doing decreases, and the very life of Christ in me increases. Biblical meditation draws me into a deeper place of adoration and worship, and positions my soul to listen, hear and yield to truth that transforms me.*

I need to share a cautionary word about this matter of hearing God's voice. We've all heard someone say, "God told me" this or that, when the fruit of their life is just not consistent with either the Word or character of the Lord. While encouraging the value of meditation, we must guard against the error of subjectivity, or hearing what I want to hear. Paul's word in 2 Timothy 2:15 is relevant here. We must handle the Word of God correctly.

We must learn to discern God's voice out of the context of the whole counsel of His mind and will throughout Scripture. We must resist the temptation to pull isolated verses out of context, or bend or twist them to suit our own need. God will never speak anything to us contrary to His Word or character. Also, the accuracy of God's leading must be discerned in community. I need to be open to submit what I perceive God to be saying to me to other trusted mentors in my life.

Meditating on His Word

As we meditate, we ask such questions as: What am I learning about God's character? What is He revealing to me about myself? Is there a teaching I need to follow? What new spiritual desires are surfacing in me? Am I living in light of this truth?

Some days the Lord seems to speak with thunder to our souls. But most days His voice sounds like a gentle rain with words of love, correction and guidance. Each encounter with Him is unique.

What do we do with distractions that come to our minds? We all find that as we come to meditate on Scripture, all kinds of distractions come to our minds and emotions. Some are easily put aside by writing them down on an "offload list" (things to buy, things to do, people to contact, e-mails or texts to respond to, and so on), and then returning to your passage. Sometimes reading and praying aloud is helpful. It slows us down and keeps us focused. Many times distractions persist. What do we do then? We need to look within to see what the real issue is. He is bringing revelation, light into our darkness. Psalm 119:30 says, "The unfolding of your words gives light, it gives understanding to the simple." The Scripture may have revealed or triggered feelings or thoughts in your conscious or unconscious mind that are real issues you need to deal with. We should never hold back our desires, feelings or negative thoughts, but express honestly whatever is on our hearts. We see this modeled in the transparent expressions of the Psalmists. *These distractions become our prayer response to God.* We dialogue with Him, interacting with the light of Scripture He has brought to us. It is here where we meet Him personally, come to know His unconditional love, and experience deeper faith and hope for personal transformation.

So how are we to meditate on God's word "day and night? " Paul instructs us, "Let the word of God dwell in you richly" (Col. 3:16). There are so many creative ways we can do this. What have *you* experienced? What comes to *your* mind when you think of doing this?

I find that I remain focused on the same Scripture throughout the day, sometimes for a week, even over a month. I keep it before me, reviewing and applying it in my daily thought processes and interactions. Sometimes I'll paraphrase it, or choose a key phrase, or make it into a summary statement. I want the essence of this truth to dwell in my mind while I am engaged in life activities. I pray the Scripture until it becomes *my* prayer...and many times I use it as I pray for others. Whatever pasture I am in that day, I am grazing on this Scripture!

The Lord will lead you as you allow His word to dwell *richly* in you every day and night. May His truth become the joy of your heart. And at night, as you rest your head on your pillow, may those times when He quickened His Word to you become what you look back on and count as the highlight of your day—because they connected you to Jesus.

Taking Time to Reflect

1. Can you think of a point in your journey when the Lord has used a particular Scripture to speak to you, resulting in change in a specific area of your life? What initiatives did you take that released the power of the Word into your life? Write these out.

2. Memorize Hebrews 4:12, then meditate on it "24/7." Let this profound truth about the transforming power of God's Word really become part of your thinking.

3. When you take time to soak in the Word, what seems to distract you the most? Random thoughts? Projects pending? Emotions up, down, all-around? Set up your own "offload list," and begin using it during your times set apart for meditation and prayer.

4. If meditation is a relatively new discipline for you, begin by putting it into practice. After you've read through these chapters on meditation, you can apply what you're learning. Commit to do at least one meditation exercise in the coming week. You may want to start by using my simplified format in the next section, Biblical Meditation: Simple Steps. I encourage you to "soak" in one passage for a few days, even the whole week!

BIBLICAL MEDITATION
Simple Steps

As you meditate on God's word, it's most important to remember that it's not any particular method you use, but rather coming with a humble, teachable heart. As you come, each interaction with Him will be different. There's no set pattern, way or form. The Holy Spirit will lead you. Sometimes your mind may wander, or fatigue overcome you. But never judge your time with Him based on what you might think or feel. Rest in the truth that He has been present with you.

Come with a sense of wonder, curiosity, and expectation as you meet with the God of the universe! He waits for you to come and hear his personal word to you! As you prepare, consider the following ways to meet with him.

Preparing Your Heart
Prayer that lead you into His presence, and keeps you there

You may want to light a candle, inviting and welcoming the light of His presence. Take a moment of silence, draw several deep breaths, allowing your thoughts and preoccupations to gear down and settle. Speak out slowly, and repeat this verse several times, allowing a moment of silence between each recitation:

> *Be still, and know that I am God.*
> Psalm 46:10

Acknowledge that God is already present to meet you where you are, as you are. *"Lord, where can I go from your spirit? "(Psalm 139:7).* Welcome Him as Immanuel, "The Lord is *with* me."

Invite Him to bring to light any distractions you may have that hinder you from receiving from Him. If necessary, confess any sin, and receive forgiveness and cleansing. Release your present cares and burdens. Ask Him to "hold" these for you, so you can be attentive. You might imagine handing off a heavy backpack for Him to hold, and carry! If you find your mind distracted with things to do, writing them down on that "offload list" I've mentioned can be helpful.

Come before the Lord with an expectant faith. Prepare to listen for, and hear, His voice. *"He wakens me morning by morning, wakens my ear to listen like one being taught." (Is 50:4).*

Soaking in His Word

Letting the Word of God irrigate the soil of your heart

Select a passage for meditation. Read it through slowly. As you read, notice what you are being drawn to: certain words, phrases, images, perhaps a person you identify or resonate with.

You may want to cross reference or compare this reading to other passages where a similar truth is revealed. Then read the passage again, slowly. Ask yourself:

"Lord, what are you revealing to me in this Scripture?"

The reading may have evoked feelings, thoughts, mental images, desires, or questions. Take some moments to pause, ponder, and reflect on ways He is beginning to get your attention. If your mind wonders, return your focus to Christ, to the truths the Spirit has highlighted to you, or re-focus on Psalm 46:10.

Listening to the Lord

Actively listening, and expecting that He will reveal Himself

Read the passage again.

"Lord, what are you speaking to me?"

Pause, notice, listen… Dialogue with Him. He may reveal more of His character and ways. You may also notice what He is revealing to you about yourself (remembering that He is for you!). Questions may surface, such as: Lord, what do you see in my heart? Is there a teaching here to follow? Are there new, godly desires stirring in me?

As you are noticing what is surfacing in you, spend time listening to the Spirit. You may want to read the passage again. Do not rush this. There is no hurry. *Meditate— soak in and dwell—on what he is speaking to you in this passage. You do not want to miss encountering Him in a personal way.*

Responding to the Lord
When God's Word becomes personalized and internalized

Consider reading your passage again. In prayer, dialogue with the Lord over what He is revealing to you. You might ask, *"What are you asking me to consider? What are you inviting me into? How can I cooperate with your Spirit?"*

Be silent, listening for His still, small voice. Notice what comes to you, so you can respond to His invitation. How have you sensed His love and encouragement to you in this time? Express that to Him.

Sometimes it's helpful to note or journal what the Lord has spoken or imparted to you. You may also write it on a card and put it in a place where you can see it often. This will stir your heart to keep turning to Him by remembering His personal word to you. Throughout the week ahead, commit to meditating on this Scripture, by keeping it in sight, memorizing it, praying it, speaking it, allowing the Spirit to continue to personalize and internalize this word, enabling you to live it out, by His grace and power.

Remember: meditating on the word is the irrigation system of our souls!

A PERSONAL EXAMPLE OF MEDITATION

Example One

As I share a personal illustration of meditating in the Word, keep in mind that I am using as my guide the four steps already shared in the previous chapter, Biblical Meditation: Simple Steps.

Preparing Your Heart

I always begin my time of meditation in God's Word by preparing my heart, acknowledging He is with me, yielding and positioning myself to focus on Him and listen.

Soaking in His Word

When approaching a portion of the Word of God, I like to spend time "soaking" in a particular passage, by reading it several times, letting it deeply irrigate the soil of my heart.

Several years ago, while continuing my quiet time in Hebrews, the Lord spoke to me powerfully. As I was reading slowly through chapter 3, He caught my attention by highlighting the following verses:

*Today, if you hear his voice do not **harden** your hearts as you did in the rebellion (wilderness).*

See to it that none of you has a sinful, unbelieving heart that turns away from the living God...
*Today, if you hear his voice, do not **harden** your hearts.*

In my heart, a question arose. How had the Israelites done this? *How* had they hardened their hearts? What were the consequences? I searched out cross references and discovered that the Israelites had quarreled with the

Lord, not trusting his clear word... they were testing him, saying, "Is the Lord among us or not?"

I read again the Hebrews portion, *"Today, if you hear his voice, do not **harden** your heart."* As I would naturally expect, the picture of a large rock came to mind...solid, hard, cold... and rain was falling on it, but no moisture was being absorbed. *Then I took this Scripture and formed it into a prayer:*

"Lord, have I hardened my heart in any way towards you?"

Listening to the Lord

I continued to meditate on the passage, reflecting on God's character. I was struck by how deeply the Israelites' sin grieved Him:

*"O Lord, what do you see in **my** heart that grieves you?"*

With an open, honest heart, I listened to the still, small voice of the Holy Spirit. I realized that I had been distancing myself from the Lord. I had been working through some disappointments, and was also feeling personal failure. As a result, I had "pulled away."

As I continued in my conversation with the Lord, I agreed with Him about the condition of my heart. He had been coming to me and speaking many times about His love, but like water being poured on a rock, my heart would not receive. Again, the verse spoke to me, *"**Do not harden your heart.**"* I began responding:

"Lord, I don't want a cold, hardened heart.
I want my heart to be like a sponge."

He then went on to reveal more of my "hard places." I read the passage again slowly, reflectively, this time thanking Him for being a God who keeps reaching out to His people even when they continually turn aside. I thanked Him for loving me enough to reveal my heart, so I could again receive His love.

"Lord, I receive your love and gentle correction today."

Responding to the Lord

I journaled the truths the Lord had given me that day. Deuteronomy 4:9 says, "Only be careful, and watch yourselves closely so that you do not forget the things your eyes have seen, or let them slip from your heart as long as you live."

To help me remember, I have a little shelf in my kitchen where I put special objects that represent a truth the Lord has revealed to me, so my eyes will see them and my heart will turn to Him. That day I put a small blue sponge on my shelf, reminding me to daily keep an honest, tender heart toward my Lord, so I would be open to receive and absorb His truth and love.

The Lord is always speaking, if only we would realize it. This is the beauty of taking time to sit at His feet and meditate on what He is wanting to speak to us personally. On many days, as I meditate, I may come away with only a reminder of His character, or a simple word that speaks to my heart, or a sense of His accepting love.

A PERSONAL EXAMPLE OF MEDITATION

Example Two

As I share another personal illustration of meditating in the Word, keep in mind again that I always begin my time by preparing my heart and focusing on the Lord.

Soaking in His Word

One of my life verses is Jeremiah 30:21:

"...I will bring him near and he will come close to me,
for who is he who will devote himself to be close to me?'"
declares the Lord.

I want to devote myself to being close to my Lord. In longing for this, I was recently led to Psalm 84. After reading the Psalm through very *slowly, repeatedly,* the Holy Spirit began to highlight certain words to me:

"My soul yearns... even faints for the living God... a nest near your altar... setting my heart on pilgrimage..."

Several questions began to form in my mind. "Have I really thought and comprehended what your dwelling place is like?" I recalled passages that spoke of His dwelling place, so I meditated on those Scriptures. Another question occurred to me: "Is my heart *daily set* on pilgrimage?"

I re-read slowly the first seven verses of Psalm 84, and as I was reading, the Lord brought a clear word picture to my mind. Years ago, while I was standing at the Wailing Wall in Jerusalem listening to the men and women pray in Hebrew, my attention was diverted to the sound of birds. As I looked up I saw a small bush, the only one on the entire wall. Nestled within its branches was a little nest holding young birds. The Lord was speaking to me.

My immediate longing was to be like those nested birds I had seen. The

Lord brought the words of the psalmist alive to my spirit —

Even the sparrow has found a home,
the swallow a nest for herself, where she may have her young
— a place near your altar...

I sat in silence before the Lord, marveling over how He was speaking to me and how He put the word picture and that Scripture together. *"Thank You, Lord."*

Listening to the Lord

I read the first seven verses of Psalm 84 over again slowly, asking, "Lord, what are you saying to me?" I wrote down several things I had learned about His character, one of which was that He is a God who blesses those who *set* their hearts on pilgrimage. I loved that word picture! That daily pilgrimage is simply experientially to know and walk with Jesus. I pondered what that would look like for me.

I asked the Lord, "What do you see in my heart?" Trying to be honest with myself, I listened for the whispers of the Spirit. I realized I had been overly restless, worrying and fretting... not longing, seeking and crying out for Him. What was robbing me of resting in Him?

As I sat in a moment of holy conversation with my Lord, I agreed with Him about the condition of my heart. I had a deep longing to be like those little sparrows: near to His altar, so dependent, trusting and resting. It was then that the Spirit of God brought this thought to me...

"Terri, make a nest where your heart can rest."

"Yes," my heart responded, "every day I need to sit at your feet, and dwell in your Word (my nest) and in the truth of *who You are*, Lord. And then throughout the day even as circumstances come and my mind wanders... my heart will *know* a resting place where I will be drawn to come and abide with you."

As I read the passage again slowly, I took time to *listen* and *receive* His love for me. "You long, O Lord, to share your dwelling place with Me! You want Me to come to you." I recalled the passage in which Jesus expressed His heart's longing for His people to come to Him: "O that I would have gathered you in my arms but you would not come" (Matt 23:37). You are a Lord who wants me near to you, even more than I long for you. *I receive Your invitation today, My Lord, to come.*

Responding to the Lord

Again, I spent time journaling the truths He had given me. That day I put on the special shelf in my kitchen a little bird's nest with a red painted heart inside it, with my name on it. Next to it is written, *"Make a nest where your heart can rest."* It is a reminder each day to set my heart on pilgrimage, to seek Him by soaking in His Word and presence. As a result, I have internalized and personalized His Word.

Make a nest...
where your heart
can rest.
∻ ♡ ∻

PRACTICING LECTIO DIVINA

Understanding Lectio Divina

Let's reflect back on our overview of biblical meditation, where I shared an introduction to the practice of lectio divina. This is a *defined approach* for personally encountering the Lord in Scripture introduced in the 6th century, but more fully developed by Ignatius in the 16th century.

"Lectio divina" is Latin for "sacred, divine reading, " a time set apart to allow Scripture to inform our thinking and listening. This is different from Bible study, where we engage in Scripture to glean insight and content. Lectio is not about getting **information** (knowledge we receive from Scripture). It is about **revelation** (a new heart understanding) that positions us for **transformation** (actual life change). As we practice lectio and *slowly, reflectively* soak in the Word, we are moved from head knowledge to heart change. We engage and respond not only with our minds, but also with our hearts, emotions, will and imagination. Since our primary objective is not to gain increased knowledge, but to deepen our intimacy with God, our singular focus becomes listening, noticing our soul condition and responses as we sit with Him and His Word.

We choose to slow down, making uncluttered space so we can pay attention to our souls. *In lectio, instead of just reading the Word, we allow the Word of God to "read us."* We do not "rush through" a passage. We let it sink into our soul and life. *In lectio we choose smaller portions of Scripture,* with the intent of slowly reading and reflecting several times through the passage, noticing what words, phrases, images we are drawn to. And we ask *"soul questions"* in response to what we have heard, without judging ourselves. Questions like these:

> As I read, what is being evoked in me? I notice my thoughts and emotions, where I find myself resonating, resisting, surprised, delighting. Why was I drawn to this word or phrase?

> How is the Lord addressing me, or getting my attention?

What are my reactions/responses telling me about where I am, the condition of my soul, my relationship to others, and where I need and long to grow in Christlikeness?

We prayerfully listen for God's voice, as we let Him be a part of our reflection, giving Him access to our hidden life, encountering Him as He speaks to and invites us into deeper relationship. We close our lectio time by resting in His unconditional love.

In lectio, we notice and make space to pause and listen. We dialogue with the Lord, then pause and listen again. Lectio is not so much a way of reading as it is a way of prayerful listening. You are allowing the Scripture to inform your thinking and move you into prayerful conversation and encounter with Him. *The essence of this practice is to listen to Scripture with the ears of one's heart, using our emotions, senses and imagination.* We are open, aware, receptive and willing, noticing our heart responses. Watch for the Holy Spirit to quicken and bring alive familiar passages in fresh ways!

Here are the steps Ignatius has given for practicing lectio:

SILENCE — "silencio,"preparing my heart to hear

READ — "lectio," listening with my heart

REFLECT — "meditatio,"going deeper in God's personal word to me

RESPOND — "oratio," letting God know in prayer how I feel

REST — "contemplatio,"returning and resting in His unconditional love

Many times our stumbling block is that we have pre-conceived ideas about familiar passages. We need to release those. Make it your focus to lean into and listen to what this Word is saying to you, ***here…now. Fresh manna!*** Allow yourself to notice how the Word is stirring and touching your inner spirit, awakening you to see Him and your heart in a new way. Sometimes in this meditation time we can feel uncomfortable with the quiet, and with what surfaces in us, as we see and present our true self to God. But the Lord longs to meet us where we *are*, not where we think or feel we *should* be. In this place of increased self-awareness and vulnerability, we encounter Jesus, and receive a personal word. He is our perfect ***"soul guide"*** who intimately knows us and gently leads us to experience the power of his transformational love.

As you begin this time listening and meditating, it is important to remember two truths. First, the Lord is your **advocate,** not your adversary. He is *for* you. Ask the Holy Spirit to increase your capacity to better discern His voice from your voice (speaking criticism or condemnation) and the voice of the enemy (accusation). Second, you're in the presence of the one who knows you, sees you and loves you. He is not judging you, but drawing and inviting you into who you really want to be, and into a deeper place of communion with Him.

In the next section, there are some lectio steps that will enable you to approach God's Word with a listening heart. While these steps can be a helpful structure, feel free to be fluid in applying them, allowing the Spirit to guide you in this encounter.

Let's also understand that lectio is not just a passive "quiet time." It is, rather, full of expectant alertness...encountering the Shepherd of your soul, receiving a personal "now" word. Even if it seems to you in lectio "nothing happened," you end with resting and remembering your true identity of being His beloved. *Just being with Him is enough.*

Practicing lectio is not just a practice I do in the morning, but I let this Word *irrigate my soul* and open my eyes to reflect, notice, and be attentive to His presence throughout the day. Sometimes I remain in my passage for days, a week, even a month, until it is internalized and living through me, continually praying through the Scripture. I have used breath prayers formed from my lectio. Sometimes I use symbols or objects that keep me returning to the truth He showed me. You can ask the Lord for creative ways you can daily keep this lectio irrigating *your* soul. *Over time I notice I've been transformed from walking a restless, distracted life to a daily life more connected, centered on the Lord, and intentionally bringing His light and life into the vineyard He has called me to work in.*

Practicing Lectio Divina

SILENCE — "silencio,"preparing my heart to hear

Begin your lectio by finding a quiet, non-distracted space. You can light a candle, as a reminder that Christ is present here with you! Take several deep breaths, sit in silence. Welcome and invite the light of God's presence.

As you quiet your heart, notice the sources of noise in your interior life. Release any distractions or burdens that would hinder you from hearing His voice or encountering His presence. Ask Him to hold these for you. Let yourself be addressed by God. Release any pre-conceived ideas you have of the passage, ready to receive.

Invite the Lord to speak afresh into your life. Open your heart to listen by slowly praying a breath prayer, such as:

* "Speak Lord, for your servant is listening."
* "Open the eyes/ears of my heart, Lord."
* "Lord, I give you permission to cultivate the soil of my heart."
* "Lord, I am here. You have my full attention. I am listening."

READ — "lectio," listening with my heart

Select a short passage. It's best if you can have a journal or hard copy to work with and write on. You are now going to begin to slow down your mental gears and focus by reading this passage in an *unhurried* way, as many times as you desire.

Read the passage slowly. As you read, notice particular words, phrases or images that seem highlighted to you, cause you to pause or slow down, capture your attention, or seem personally addressed to you. The Spirit is beginning to draw you. Mark what stands out to you. Do not analyze or judge or try to figure out *why* it has your attention. Just quietly dwell with these words, allowing them to turn over in your mind and heart. *Simply notice what you're noticing.* Take as much time as you feel you need before moving on.

REFLECT — "meditatio,"going deeper in God's personal word to me

Read the passage again, more reflectively (you may want to read another translation, or a paraphrase, like the Message, or Amplified Bible). As you read, you're going to let the Word probe more deeply under the surface of your soul, reflecting now on why these particular words, phrases or images stood out to you, what they bring to your mind, and how they connect to your life today.

Read the passage again, slowly. As you read, notice your thoughts, emotions and heart responses, positive or negative. You may also ask or notice:

Why was I drawn to these particular words/phrases/images?

What is this passage evoking, stirring or surfacing in me? Perhaps an impression, a resistance, a longing, something that draws, disturbs or delights me.

Notice your emotional reactions/responses. *Why am I responding this way? Lord, where are you getting my attention, and why?*

How is this passage connecting or resonating with my life right now? (What part of my life needs to hear this today?)

Take a moment. *Sit and quiet your own words and thoughts.* Listen to what comes to you. You may want to note any specific impressions, emotions, or gentle whispers as you allow God's Word to speak to and *"read you."*

Pause again, and listen. As the Spirit is bringing something to your attention, *just stop, linger, stay there. Do not move on until you sense you are ready.* More revelation may come. You might read the passage again. Take time to ponder on what He is revealing to you.

We all have a tendency to be quick to move on to the next thing. We need to learn to stay/remain with what delights, bothers, or stirs us, so this meditation can become a transforming encounter with the Lord.

RESPOND — "oratio," letting God know in prayer how I feel

This is my *inner response* in prayer, a personal dialogue with the Lord. I notice the prayers that are surfacing in me as I bring to Him what I've been feeling and reflecting on.

Read the passage again slowly, and ask the Lord, *"What are you inviting me into, or towards?"* Perhaps it is a personal invitation to grow in Christlikeness, to meditate on His love, repent, release, lament, something to act on, or something to give God praise and thanksgiving for.

Pause and listen. Dialogue and process your responses *honestly* with the Lord. Sometimes this is a place of struggle or wrestling. *Don't rush this,* and don't be critical of yourself. Give yourself grace.

Ask the Lord, *"What next steps are you inviting me to take to walk this out"?* (Remember, one small, simple step of obedience can change the trajectory of your soul!) Again, take time to listen.

Through my obedience, the Word takes root in the soil of my soul and bears fruit. This is where I am intentional, surrendering and allowing Him to integrate what He has shown me, and implement it into my daily life.

REST — "contemplatio,"returning and resting in His unconditional love

In these moments, the Lord invites you to return to a place of stillness, to receive rest. "Like a weaned child is my soul within me" (Psalm 131:2). Content just to be with your Maker.

"Lord, I receive your rest and unconditional love."

Take a deep breath. Inhale, then exhale…slowly. Still your mind from all you've been processing. *Just be with, and behold the Lord.* Allow your soul to soak in, receive, and reflect on His personal affirmation and unconditional love for you.

My soul finds rest in God alone.

—Psalm 62:1

You may ask the Lord for a breath prayer from this time that will keep you centered and returning to Him. Most importantly, meditate on your lectio through the week by keeping it before you and praying through it. *The purpose of His transforming work in me is that it should impact my life, my relationships and that which He has called me to do.*

In the Appendix, you will find a list of short passages that can be used for lectio.

LECTIO DIVINA –
Short Version

We do lectio in an unhurried way, using small portions of Scripture.

STEP 1: Heart Preparation
~ Find a quiet place.
~ Take some deep breaths.
~ You might light a candle, and welcome the Lord's presence.
~ Come expectant, that He will speak personally to you.
~ Pray: "Lord, I am here, attentive, and listening for a fresh 'now word' from You."

STEP 2: Read (listening with my heart)
~ Slowly read the passage through, without stopping.
~ As you read, notice particular words, phrases, or images that seem highlighted to you, cause you to pause, or seem addressed to you. Circle or underline them. Don't analyze or try to figure out why you are drawn to these. Spend a few moments dwelling on them, allowing them to slowly settle into your heart and mind.

STEP 3: Reflect (going deeper in God's personal Word to me)
~ Explore now more deeply, reflecting on why you were drawn to these words/ phrases/images, and any other way the Lord may be personally addressing you.
~ Read the passage again, unhurried, this time perhaps in a different translation. Notice what is stirring or surfacing in you. How is the Holy Spirit getting your attention? *Notice your thoughts and emotional responses.* Lord, what do you want me to know about myself, or about You? How is this passage resonating or connecting with your life *right now?* Pause, take time to ponder the word, phrase or image in your heart, and what it means to you.

STEP 4: Respond (letting God know in prayer how I feel)
~ Read the passage again, then move into a personal dialogue with the Lord, pouring out your heart response to His Word spoken to you. Notice the prayers rising in you. You might engage with the Lord over these questions: "What are you inviting me into? Is there anything I want to hold in my heart from this time? How are You inviting me to walk out what You are revealing to me?"

STEP 5: Rest (returning and resting in His unconditional love)
~ In these moments, the Lord invites you to return to a place of stillness, to receive rest, and just *be* with Him. There is no need for words. Take several deep breaths, quieting your mind and emotions, receiving and soaking in His unconditional love and soul rest for you. Now carry this into your day.

LECTIO –
A Personal Example

I'd like to share with you a lectio divina I did some years ago. This is an example of how the Lord uses a passage or truth already familiar to me to bring a deeper revelation of that truth to my soul, through His Spirit.

I began, as I typically do, lighting a candle, calming my spirit, and focusing on the light of His presence with me. This is a familiar passage. I release my pre-conceived thoughts, and ask the Lord to open the eyes of my heart, bringing a fresh word to my soul. "Speak, Lord, for your servant is listening" (Samuel).

I read Isaiah 49:14-16. Here's the context. God's people are dealing with the painful realities of captivity. The Lord is pouring out His heart of compassion towards them, expressing His covenantal commitment to restore His relationship with them: "Shout for joy, O heavens; rejoice O earth; burst into song, O mountains! For the Lord comforts His people and will have compassion on his afflicted ones." Beautiful, heartfelt words of loving commitment. But now here's the *but:*

But Zion has said, 'The Lord has forsaken me,
and my Lord has forgotten me.'
Can a mother forget her nursing child
and not have compassion on the son of her womb?
Surely they may forget, yet I will not forget you.
See, I have inscribed you on the palms of my hands;
your walls are continually before me.
NKJV

I read this portion slowly, **noticing what words, phrases or images caught my attention, or began to draw my heart.** For me, these words: "forgotten… forget…" A single phrase, "can a mother forget?"

I sat for a few moments with this image of a mother nursing her baby. Then I began turning these words over in my mind, "never forget," letting them settle from my head into my heart. I sat in stillness.

I read the passage again in a different translation, ***noticing my thoughts, emotions and heart responses:***

But Zion (Jerusalem in captivity) said,
"The Lord has abandoned me, and my Lord has forgotten me."
(The Lord answered) "Can a woman forget her nursing child and have
no compassion on the son of her womb?
Even these may forget, but I will not forget you.
Indeed, I have inscribed (a picture of) you on the palms of My hands;
your city walls, Zion, are continually before Me."

Amplified

I kept noticing what was being evoked in me. I found myself *identifying and resonating* with these Israelites. I began honestly processing and dialoguing with the Lord. "Lord, I'm remembering a recent time when You *seemed* quiet, un-attentive and non-responsive to my feelings and prayers. My mind and past experiences knew these responses about who You are, were *not* accurate. But emotionally at times I felt different. I hear the Israelites pour out this same complaint, but I notice You listened and did not judge them. You were not harsh. Instead, You gave them the most intimate, tender image of Your love for them, by saying to them, '*Can a mother forget her nursing child and not have compassion on the son of her womb*'"?

Lord, what do You want me to know?

I pondered this, continuing my dialogue with the Lord. "It's true, a mother *may* forget, be neglectful and unattached, but what I hear you saying to me: My love for you is of a magnitude beyond even the most nurturing, attentive, sacrificial, intimate love a mother has for her baby. Not only that, but beyond that, ***I will never forget you! And everything about My nature is turned toward you with compassion.*** " That was so much for me to fully comprehend!"

I paused to reflect.

The memory surfaced in me when I had my first child, and how life-transforming this was. Day and night, 24/7, he was always on my mind. My life revolved around him. Even when I went to sleep, I was never un-mindful of him.

Again, I sat with this, letting the Lord reveal what this meant, then…letting it soak into my heart, where I could *feel* the reality of what He was saying here: "My love is **beyond** a mother's love. Terri…I will never forget *you*." Inwardly, I slowly repeated those words several times.

I read the passage again, listening and noticing what else might surface. We dialogued together. These words came: *"You, Terri, are engraved in My hand, My love is permanent. Your walls are ever before Me."* I paused, listened again, and responded. "Lord, there is a personal 'Terri wall' of my everyday life that is always before You! You know where I am…You know my limitations…I am always on Your mind!"

I soaked in these words of truth, and sensed He was inviting me to just be still and listen while He spoke them personally *to* and *over* me.

This encounter went even deeper, even though I had been *familiar* with these truths, God's Spirit was supernaturally moving them from my head and deeper into my heart. I was beholding the beauty of the Lord! *It was one thing to know that I am seen, known and loved by my Lord, but that He would never forget me was a different aspect of His love to know and internalize.*

Lord, what are you inviting me into?

The following came to me: You are reminding me that You welcome and take to heart all my meandering thoughts in my ordinary days and my desert wanderings when I struggle to understand Your ways. I realized there are times that I can let how I feel shape my perception of who You are and also during seasons when you may seem quiet and non-responsive, even though I know that's not true. I was so comforted by Your tender response to the Israelites in their similar struggle, revealing Your "mother's kind of heart" to them. I love how You are a God who took a most significant image of a mother's love they have known or seen to help them be able to understand more of Your true heart towards them. You long to make Yourself known. I want to become more aware and notice the ways You use images to help me see and understand You. My soul finds rest as I meditate on and journal the words and images You drew me to today. Your love is a permanent, anchored love—always fully attentive with immeasurable compassion, and intimately and deeply bonded to me, the one You created.

***Lord, is there a breath prayer that you have for me
from this time with you?***

I took unhurried time to listen for what emerged from my heart.

"Lord, I am anchored in Your love."

"Lord, my 'Terri wall' is ever before you."

I lingered, letting go of my mental processing, just resting in His presence, soaking in His love.

As I sat, several friends came to my mind that were going through pain and heartache, and expressing the struggle of feeling like the Israelites when the Lord seemed distant, and they felt forgotten. I sensed Him inviting me to text them this passage, and as they come to mind, to pray this Scripture for them.

I still return often to this passage, always delighted and surprised how such familiar truth continues to speak and deepen in me. Each time I have encountered the Lord bringing more revelation, deepening my relationship with Him, and experiencing transformation in my own soul. I keep this Scripture written out where I can see, meditate, and pray through it. Throughout the day, as I'm led, I have used these breath prayers to re-center my mind and heart, as they bring such reminders of the intimacy and incomprehensible depth of His love for me. And I have been prompted many times to share this Scripture with others.

I believe the Lord has fresh "soul manna" for each of us to partake of. Come to His table through lectio meditation, and do not miss the "soul feast" He has prepared for you.

When your words came, I ate them;
they were my joy and my heart's delight,
for I bear your name, Lord God Almighty.
—Jeremiah 15:16

SABBATHS OF THE HEART

I want to introduce to you a personal practice that has helped me build purposeful pauses into the pace of my life, enabling me to grow in my attentiveness to Jesus. One day the Lord gave me an image that captures these moments when I stop and hit the pause button. I call these *"sabbaths of the heart."* At any moment, in any circumstance, I can employ one or more of the spiritual disciplines: drawing near to God, finding an opportunity for solitude, speaking a breath prayer, or pausing to behold His beauty.

Sabbaths of the heart are intentional and internal rhythms/practices I do that keep me centered and companioning with Jesus. They are invitations throughout my day to enter more deeply into intimacy with Him. They keep me aware of and noticing His presence. I offer Him the gift of my attention, and access to my soul. These pauses prompt me to say, "Lord, I am present." They are ways of cultivating a listening heart.

Throughout the Old Testament, we see Yahweh revealing a profound relational desire to dwell with those He has chosen. *The root meaning of "dwell" is to inhabit, take up permanent residence, to settle down, be at home.* I love the way He expresses this through his prophet Joel when the Israelites were in a dark time in their history, devastated by an army of locusts. Even after painful rounds of rebellion and disobedience, He shares this:

Never again will my people be despised.
*You'll know without question that I'm in the **thick of life** with Israel, that I'm your God, yes, your God, the one and only real God. Never again will my people be despised.*

— Joel 2:27 (The Message)

As a covenantal, relational Creator, He proved over and over His desire and faithfulness to dwell and be in the midst of His people. We can rest in the assurance that our God wants to be *with* us even in the messy and miraculous moments of our faith journeys. Here are some questions I often ask myself: how do I get more consistent dwelling *with Him? **How do I cultivate a heart of attentiveness centered on being present in His presence?** How do

I abide with Jesus in my busy, distracted life? I find there is truly a "Mary and Martha" within me (Luke 10:38-42). Martha got distracted, getting caught up in her tasks ("doing"). Mary chose to quiet herself, and sit at the Master's feet ("being"). I need to nurture more of the "Mary" in me. It's so easy for me to live day by day not wanting "my agenda" to be interrupted.

Practicing God's presence is about being open to inviting Him *into* my everyday moments, pausing to listen for His voice, watching for and noticing the gentle promptings, goodness, and invitations from the One who vigilantly keeps watch over me. I have the moment by moment, day by day *choice* to respond to His desire and design to dwell with me. As I make even small heart movements towards Him, these pauses become windows through which I see and receive grace *(celebrate your small steps!)*. It is my part to be intentional to build into my walk practices and rhythms that enable me to more closely companion with Jesus.

We're all familiar with this profound line from one of the sons of Korah, Psalm 46:10:

"Be still and know that I am God."

The implication is clear—there is a connection between being still, and knowing Him more deeply. I love the imagery from the Message paraphrase: "Step out of the traffic! Take a long, loving look at me, your High God." *Sabbaths of the heart can happen when we choose to "step out of the traffic" of our busy, distracted lives and make space to re-center our souls, being drawn into His always available presence.*

Simply stated, you are choosing to pause, and pay attention.

I have found a sabbath of the heart in the flow of my day can take on many creative and varied rhythms and forms. You can ask the Lord to show you what this looks like in *your* life. It can be making a "rest stop" by slowing down your gears, hitting the pause button, and finding a quiet place to take some moments to engage God's Word, or just be quiet with Him. While in nature, it could be actually stopping to savor the gift of His incredible creation. It might be taking a moment to pause in your day and notice what you are enjoying and delighting in. It could be a re-set of your mind or emotions through a breath prayer, or doing an examen for a few moments at the end of your day. When driving, I sometimes follow a rhythm of using road signs to guide my praying. For example, slowing down passing by a school, and praying for children. Or, "Reduce Speed," slowing down my mind and emotions and inviting the Spirit to prompt prayers in me. Or "Yield," intentionally inviting the Lord into my current circumstance. Scriptures I'm meditating on are placed in my home and prompt me to pause and draw near. Sabbaths of the heart can look like a rhythm to pause to pray each morning, noon and night.

Throughout the day, I seem to find many reflective moments or "mini-Sabbath windows" where I pause and inquire of the Lord with these two questions, which keep me listening and attentive to Him: *"Lord, what do you want me to know right now? What are you inviting me into?"* These questions bring to me awareness and revelation that often result in immediate change in my perspective or responses. Sabbaths of the heart are ways I nurture the "Mary" in me, by choosing to pause and listen.

As I put these simple disciplines into practice, I have found these sabbaths of the heart enable me to become more aware of the presence of Immanuel, the Lord *dwelling "with me!"* As I choose to slow down and break out of my "Terri mindset" and place my soul in His presence, He captures my attention, and speaks to my heart. This always feels like I am "coming home" again as I am awakened to who and whose I really am.

As you read through and reflect on the sections ahead, I encourage you to simply begin noticing fresh openings or opportunities in the day-to-days of your journey to pause and build into your walk with Jesus these life-giving sabbaths of *your* heart.

PRAYERS OF THE HEART

Having explored the principles and practices of some of the core spiritual disciplines, I'd like now to briefly introduce a few additional prayer practices that help us more consistently practice living in God's presence.

There are many names and expressions for a variety of prayer practices we may engage in: meditative prayer, "praying the Scriptures," listening prayer, intercession, petition, fixed hour prayer, and more. Of course all of these engage our heart, mind and emotions. Even though we have times of silence and listening with these expressions, we typically use words as we connect with the Lord. Praying like this requires a focus of thoughts and a framing of words.

First, some observations about centering prayer. This is an intentional framing of simple words, a phrase, a Scripture or an image that expresses the intent or desire of my heart to be with God. This "sacred prayer word" is very personal. We spend time with the Lord to notice our personal words, such as: "My soul rests; My Shepherd; Peace, be still." It can also be speaking a name of God. Predominantly, in moments of solitude, I speak these simple words when my mind and emotions wander, re-centering my soul.

Centering prayer can also be practiced during and throughout our busy days when we get distracted, feel anxious, stressed, or want to re-connect with His presence. Expressing our "sacred word" simply brings our souls back to that place of deep abiding.

In Scripture, we see God getting the attention of ordinary people engaged in everyday tasks, like getting water at a well, stomping grapes, sweating in a wine press, or tending sheep. For you and me, this might be doing errands, preparing meals, traveling through an airport, or sitting in a hospital waiting room. The goal is that throughout the day, as the noises and activities of life invade my inner world, I can be drawn in those moments to return to my secret place, where I continually experience His attentive presence and voice, even in the middle of my daily circumstances!

Some years back, I made this card and placed it on my kitchen shelf to remind me to continually turn my thoughts back to the Lord. We're all familiar with the common road sign for a U-turn. This is an ordinary, everyday sign. May this card serve as a supernatural reminder to recognize when you are misdirected, employ a "centering prayer", and turn back toward Christ.

With this picture of the U-turn in mind, ask yourself, where is my "Center?" May I suggest it is that secret place in your heart where the Holy Spirit indwells your spirit, a place of deepest union with God. That's your core, the real you, where you know who and Whose you are. In short, centering prayer will help you to either turn towards "home" anytime, or return "home" from any distraction or circumstance that pulls you "off-center".

In the language of navigation, this is the work of a gyroscope, a finely tuned instrument that keeps you balanced, and moving in the right direction. I recommend the use of a single centering word or phrase, like looking for that U-turn sign when driving in the wrong direction! *"Return to your rest, O my soul" (Psalm 16:7).*

Let me now share a few thoughts about a very special kind of prayer of the heart, contemplative prayer, where we experience a deeper level of heart-to-heart encounter with God, often involving few words, sometimes no words at all.

Contemplative prayer opens a door for a relational union with God, setting aside agendas, needs or burdens, and just *being* with Him. As we empty ourselves in this way, and simply wait on Him, we find we are more restful in prayer. We move beyond conversation that requires words, being attentively open to Him, drawn into a place of restful communion. This is like two people who are very comfortable with each other, sitting in silence, just being together in a restful way. Words are not needed.

We experience this by making a quiet space within ourselves. Our singular aim is to *"behold"* the Lord, offering our attentiveness and affection…and letting Him *"hold"* us. This is a posture we hear expressed eloquently by David so often in the Psalms: being, waiting, resting in his presence.

Be still and know that I am God
— Psalm 46:10

My soul waits for the Lord, my soul waits
— Psalm 130:5

There are times in my life when I realize the constant flow of my thoughts and words just exhausts me, and I find myself longing to *just be in quietness* with my Lord! *I just want to stay there!* I imagine myself in Psalm 23, "He leads me beside quiet waters, he restores my soul."

As we choose to enter in and practice contemplative prayer, we find that even as we are in His presence our inner "noise" will be surfacing and feel invasive. There will be many thoughts and distractions that arise. This is normal. But we don't judge our thoughts, feelings or focus on them, or write them down. Neither do we try to push them away. It is then that we just inwardly, gently bring our hearts back to that restful posture of being with Him.

What does contemplative prayer look and feel like? As we saw earlier in the "Well-Watered Garden," David shares an image of true contemplative prayer, a soul at rest, *"I have stilled and quieted my soul; like a weaned child with its mother, like a weaned child is my soul within me."* Meditating on this image draws me to desire this in my own relationship with God. I love how the weaned child is resting in his mother's presence, trusting his needs are met, and will be met. Not demanding, striving, or exerting any effort. But rather *content just to be, absorbing the warmth, resting in the arms, soaking in the assured affection and attentive presence of a caring mother.* For me, resting in this way would mean my burdens are laid aside. I don't have to figure everything out, or wonder what the future is. I do not feel the need to talk. I experience the same kind of peace that a weaned child feels in his mother's arms, being so trusting and content.

In contemplative prayer, the Lord *initiates* and opens the door of His heart to us in this way. He draws us to Himself. We become aware of and experience a distinct manifestation or sense of His presence, a restfulness, a grace gift of personal love from the Holy Spirit. When this happens, simply stay there... linger... like David's content child. Enjoy and soak in this moment. Be grateful for this precious gift of intimacy.

I encourage you to simply be open to times when you're with the Lord *"like a weaned child,"* and there's *no need to talk or do anything!* You're just content and restful in His presence. It is a way He is initiating His love towards you, a place of deep abiding.

Some suggested ways to enter into contemplative prayer:

As you begin to experience this kind of prayer, it may only last a few minutes. That's fine. We're not used to quieting ourselves in this way.

- Settle into quietness. Sit comfortably. There's nothing you need to try to make happen! ("Lord, I am here").

- As you sit in silence, notice and listen for a word, image, phrase, Scripture or name of God that expresses your intent or desire to be with Him right now ("My soul waits") This is your "prayer word." You may silently speak your prayer word as a way of saying, "I am here." Let it draw you into His presence as you wait on Him. As distractions come, re-center by gently speaking your prayer word.

- While you are still, you might become aware and notice the ways the Lord is manifesting His presence to you. Watch for grace-filled moments when the anxious thoughts and distractions seem to "fall away or fade," and you find you *are* that *"weaned child!"* Simply receive and soak in this with gratitude.

A few additional thoughts about practicing "prayers of the heart." You can of course engage these prayers in a specific time and place of solitude ("go into your closet, and shut the door"). But you can also employ prayers like this in the flow of "normal" life, what I like to call my *"portable tent of meeting," where I have continual access to Him in any circumstance.*

The Lord loves any and all of our varied heart prayers *toward* Him! My intimacy has deepened in different ways as I have chosen to meet Him by engaging in prayers of the heart. I would like to share now another prayer of the heart, one that the Lord has used to keep me abiding in Him, the breath prayer.

PRACTICING BREATH PRAYER
A Sabbath of the Heart

Having explored the practice of what we generally call "prayers of the heart," I want to explain a particular practice that has significantly changed my own interior life, the "breath prayer."

Created in the image and likeness of God, the human being is a remarkable blend of body, mind and spirit, a holistic expression of personhood. The breath prayer brings together an expression of the whole person centering on the presence of God in the flow of everyday life. The apostle Paul urges his readers:

In view of God's mercy, offer your bodies as living sacrifices to God. This is your spiritual act of worship

— Romans 12:1

Throughout the Scriptures we notice how saints use their bodies in a manner of worship that helped them focus their minds and engage their hearts: kneeling, lying prostrate, standing, raising hands, dancing, singing, shouting!

The breath prayer is one of the classic spiritual disciplines where we use our breathing to slow down and re-center on the Lord. This prayer is similar to the "sacred prayer word" I introduced earlier, helpful for a re-centering of our souls, whereas the breath prayer is practiced in association with our pattern of breathing. It is not mindless, but rooted in Scripture, God-directed. ***It is a slow breathing of our heart longings combined with meditation on God's Word, spoken in one breath.***

It is repeated throughout the day in any given moment or circumstance, as you sense the need for a re-set or re-focus. These prayers are as simple as breathing, but slowing down, and infusing your breath with prayer. Here's an example of one I used when I desired to experience more of His nearness throughout the day:

Breathe in… *Immanuel*
Breathe out… *God with Terri (or me)*

How is a breath prayer formed? Begin by finding a quiet place and time. Identify a deep longing or heart need. A root desire that is true of where you are right now in your spiritual journey. Don't feel pressure to make anything up. Rather, discover your longing by allowing the Holy Spirit to bring to your attention what is stirring in your innermost being. Do your best to put words to it, allowing this longing to surface. Then reflect on an aspect of God's character or name of God you are drawn to, or is meaningful to you right now. Then you combine the name of God or Scripture with your specific desire, and form it into a single, short prayer phrase.

Here's the simple process:

Listen. Imagine Jesus asking you, "What do you want, or need?" (He asked the blind man, "What do you want me to do for you?") Identify what your soul truly needs or longs for right now.

Ponder: a name of God that you are drawn to and want to dwell on. Or a Scripture that expresses a personal desire.

Breathing: this is the essential part of this practice. You slowly breathe in, saying His name, then as you exhale, express your prayer.

Abba….I belong to you.

Lord… you're my waymaker.

El Roi… Lord, you see me.

Jesus… I release this to you.

Lord… my soul finds rest in you alone.

Shepherd… calm my anxious heart.

Breath prayers are one way to practice a "sabbath of the heart," an intentional pause I choose to build into the pace of my life. They are very personal. I carry prayers like this with me throughout the day, as I do household chores, while in meetings, preparing a meal, sitting in traffic…reminding my soul that the Lord is near, and attentive. I have found the Holy Spirit continually changes my perspective and responses through these prayers.

Often, a breath prayer will form and flow out of a lectio meditation where the Lord has spoken personally to me. Other times, they form as I pour my heart out to God and notice my need in that moment or circumstance of life. Practicing this kind of prayer is one way I can meditate and live out what He has revealed to me. It is so empowering and creative, enabling me to practice His presence every day.

This practice has also brought increased intimacy and inner transformation in my walk with Jesus. Sometimes I will "camp out" in a single breath prayer over a week, even a month! Let these prayers linger with you. Honestly, I'm often surprised by some of the creative, timely prayers that form out of my soul soil!

Some years back, my husband and I faced a very difficult and lengthy trial in a ministry situation. This was very painful and stressful. The Lord led me to meditate on a familiar story, Jesus in the boat with His disciples in the middle of a raging storm (Matt 8:23-26). I even used a painting of this story by Rembrandt as I reflected on this passage. Out of my lectio meditation, He gave me this simple, personal breath prayer: *"Jesus, you're in my boat."* Over several months, when heaviness and anxiety rose in me, I would breathe in, "Jesus," then breathe out, "you're in *my* boat!"

During that hard season, I didn't have to find or use a lot of words to explain or process what I was feeling. That simple phrase, "Jesus, you're in my boat" summed up an affirmation of my soul that released His provision of peace and security in a very difficult situation. As I did this breath prayer, I experienced Him ministering to me. Sometimes the heaviness would tangibly lift off, or a settled peace wash over me. *I was assured, and reminded, He was in this process with me!* And I could then trust that He was fully present in my boat and working His purpose, even in the storm.

I learned some significant things in that season. When my soul gets stressed and anxious, I can train my spirit to immediately turn to the Lord and seek His provision of peace and calm in that moment. And, "on the go and in the flow" of daily life, I can have a sabbath of my heart, slowing down my pace and receiving grace through the simple rhythm of my breath prayer.

I have discovered an amazing power in these simple breath prayers. I have found they have a "life of their own." These prayers sink deep into the crevices of our souls. They go from our heads into our hearts, where God's Spirit empowers us to live in a place of His presence, above the circumstances and emotions and stresses we find ourselves in.

So, you're probably already discovering, framing and using prayers like this in your own sojourn with Jesus. Great! Continue on. But if not, I encourage you to build this simple practice into your everyday life.

PRACTICING THE PERSONAL EXAMEN

A Sabbath of the Heart

Developed by St. Ignatius, the personal examen is a way of briefly reviewing and assessing our walk with the Lord over a day or period of time. This is a *prayerful exercise*, recalling, noticing and discerning the presence of God with us, and us with Him, in the flow of our lives.

The reality is, in this highly distracting digital age we find ourselves in, we are constantly processing information and events. How easy it is to miss what God is doing in our multiplied moments of life! We often fail, don't we, to acknowledge the presence of our unseen Shepherd alongside us, personally speaking to our souls, drawing us to Himself, opening doors for touching people's lives.

As we practice the examen, we begin to cultivate and nurture a life of intentional awareness and attentiveness to the Lord. Much of life is filled with mundane, ordinary tasks. But ask yourself this question: *What could it be like to become more discerning of God's presence throughout the day, learning and realizing ways to abide with Him?*

The examen gives us opportunity to grow in our awareness that Immanuel is with us, whether we're aware of Him or not. As we review our day, and trace "God movements" in our hearts and circumstances, we sift through a variety of feelings and impressions. Ignatius described two movements of emotion that we need to pay attention to: consolation, when I experience comfort and encouragement, and desolation, when I feel distanced from Him, or discouraged.

How do I practice personal examen?

- I like to think of this as inviting the Lord to review a "video" of my day (or week, or longer). This is a reflective look in my "rear view mirror," a sifting through the scenes in my day, not merely listing things that happened, but "comparing notes" with Him about my responses to specific situations. I might become aware of promptings, grace-filled moments, God-given desires, fingerprints of God, things to be grateful for/celebrate, conversations, or opportunities to bless others. Or, it might be missed opportunities, anxious moments, pre-occupations or distractions.

• By reviewing my day with God, I learn to see better how, when, and where He is engaging in my day. I ask questions like—What were You saying to me during and through the situations, conversations and relational encounters in my day? When did I walk in the fruits of the Spirit? How well did I love today? When did I hear Your voice today? Where did I see You working in a difficult situation?" A variety of scenes may surface—pay attention to the *one* that seems the most vivid, or pronounced. I process with Him in prayer what I'm noticing whether negative or positive. Remember, the purpose of the examen is to learn how to more consistently abide in Him. Many times I have taken what is revealed to me into an extended time of prayer, inviting the Lord to interact with me as we probe deeper.

One day reading through Luke 24, I realized this was a profound example of examen, a conversation and meal the post-Resurrection Jesus had with two unidentified people on the road to Emmaus. Jesus was walking with them, but they were unaware of who He was! They walked a long distance. They were troubled and grieving. Jesus opened up the Scriptures with them. It was not until sharing a meal, when He broke bread with them, that their eyes were opened. Then, He was gone! Here's their very unique, one-of-a-kind examen: "Were not our hearts burning with us while he talked with us on the road and opened the Scriptures to us?" (24:32).

They were reviewing this extraordinary day. They noticed a physical sensation in their bodies, a sensory "burning of their hearts." Looking back they noticed a distinct internal stirring. Something was "quickened" in them. But *at the time* it was hard to identify what that stirring was.

As they walked back to Jerusalem that night, I can only imagine their continuing conversation as they reviewed their day, realizing He was virtually present *with* them, but they were *unaware!* What a humbling realization! Was there perhaps a sense of regret? Perhaps they noticed how He was trying to get their attention as He opened the meaning of the Scripture and the prophecies about Him fulfilled. Perhaps they also noticed how He was compassionate, letting them pour out their grieving hearts to Him, and He welcomed their questions. Maybe they also noticed the desire that surfaced in them when they begged Him to please stay, not go on, and dine with them, and His graciousness to remain. Or the way their hearts changed and were filled with hope and recognized Him when He revealed Himself to them in that moment of the breaking of the bread. Might they have recalled a memory association of the bread with an experience they had heard about, or had with Him? Imagine the joy they must have felt when they realized this was Jesus. *"He was with us, the risen Lord!"*

If they hadn't reviewed their experience of that day (doing the examen) they would have missed understanding so much about the Lord, and themselves!

I truly believe that if you practice the personal examen over time, your desire to seek and abide with Him will only deepen, as the eyes of your heart are more intentionally being trained to see how He is present with you in the moments of your everyday life. You will find yourself saying more often...*"He was with me!"*

Ignatius provided a helpful pattern that many have used. Below is my own adaptation, in modern-day language. This practice can be done daily (preferred), weekly or monthly. Some find it valuable to do a yearly examen. Honestly, as you gear down at day's end, this can only take 5-10 minutes, even in bed before going to sleep.

PERSONAL EXAMEN
"Checking in with God"

Examen is a way of reflecting on the presence of God in my daily life, paying attention and noticing how he has been revealing himself as Immanuel, "God with me."

REVELATION: "Lord, open the eyes of my heart as I review my day. Help me see it through *Your* eyes" (Eph 1:18).

GRATITUDE: As you reflect, slow down and notice God's goodness. What gifts and blessings (everyday moments big and small) come to mind? Savor and express gratitude for what you feel thankful for. Did you see Him working in a difficult situation?

REVIEW : Sift through the situations/interactions of your day. Without judging yourself, take note of your emotional responses to them (joy, patience, compassion, gratitude, envy, irritation, anxiety). Try to focus on *one* aspect of the day the Lord highlights to you: a shortcoming, a prompting you acted on, a missed opportunity, a moment of regret, getting distracted, an unexpected blessing, something to celebrate. Were the fruits of the Spirit evident in me today? Did I recognize His voice?

Lord, show me when You were present and I was caught up in my own emotions or responses (distracted or resistant) and missed the awareness of You working in and through me.

Lord, show me a moment when I was aware of Your presence and how You were working in and through me as a conduit of Your love.

RESPOND/REPENT/REJOICE: In the presence of His unfailing love, name your sins/shortcomings/distractions. Confess and receive his forgiveness. Prayerfully listen and dialogue with the Lord about what He is revealing to you. Celebrate any ways you've been encouraged by seeing the Holy Spirit move or personally hearing His voice.

RENEW: Close with a moment of stillness, receiving and soaking in His unconditional, unchanging love for and delight over you (Zeph 3:17). As you think about tomorrow, what stirs in you? Is there something to pray into? Ask Him for grace to be increasingly aware of His presence, and to help you as you companion more consistently with Him.

PERSONAL EXAMEN
A Short Form

1. **Awareness of God's presence**
   - Lord, let me see my day through Your eyes.
   - When did I experience Your presence or see You moving in my day?

2. **Gratitude**
   - What am I most thankful for today?
   - Celebrate things both big and small.

3. **Review your day**
   - What was one aspect of your day that seems to stand out, and why?
   - Notice and reflect on your emotions throughout the day.
   - How did you respond to different situations?
   - Any shortcomings?
   - Lord, what do You want me to learn, or know?

4. **Reflect**
   - When were you aware you were able to serve and love others?
   - Was there a missed opportunity?
   - Did you see the fruit of the Spirit in your life today?

5. **Looking towards tomorrow**
   - What thoughts and emotions are surfacing?
   - Pray, inviting the Lord into your next day.

JOURNALING
Recording your growing intimacy with God

Friendship is the inexpressible comfort of feeling safe with a person,
having neither to weigh thoughts or measure words.
— *George Elliot*

This quotation expresses the value of my experience with journaling. I have found this to be a way that I can share and reveal the "real me" to the one who knows my innermost thoughts and ways and accepts the unedited pouring out of my heart.

Journaling can be creative and "custom-made" to fit our individual personalities. The truth is, there's no "correct way" to journal! Find the way and rhythm that fits *you*. Even those who do not like to write can find creative ways to journal. You can write short paragraphs or summary statements, draw pictures or symbols, or simply jot notes that capture your walk with God. Some have a journal of favorite quotations, Scriptures, poetry, or artwork that helps them pay attention to the work and presence of God in their lives. Personally, I have found a blessing in doing it.

Journaling can provide a kind of accountability that is helpful. It helps me involve the Lord in my daily thoughts and experiences as I record ways I want to grow in spiritual maturity. It keeps me accountable to and reminds me of what He has been speaking to me, and what I want to center and meditate on. Otherwise, I have a tendency to just move on to the next text or truth without internalizing what He has clearly shown me.

This practice also enables me to assess my life (which few of us ever take the time to do) and process soul-searching questions relevant to my spiritual growth. This can be a process of exploration in which I ask and discover where I really am in my journey with the Lord, and what I'm learning. I also love recording answers to deep prayer longings, God "surprises" and timely words for my soul.

Journaling really is a recording of my "prayer listening" heart to heart conversations with the Lord. *As I slow down my thoughts by writing, it gives me space to pause and pay attention to what I am hearing.* Sometimes I'll journal while meditating on a passage, recording my thoughts and soul responses to what the Word is stirring in me. For example, I might meditate on Psalm 23, then prayerfully record my reflections and responses, line by line.

How often one journals is, of course, an individual preference. In some seasons of my life I may journal more than others. I'm not consistent at this. But I'm grateful for having done this over the years. However often you do it, there are many benefits, the greatest of which is taking time to remember the ways in which He has moved in your life. *I love sometimes going back through this spiritual "photo album" of my life* and view both the bigger picture and the fine details of His presence in my journey. As I have reviewed my journals, I often realize how much I forget the ways He has spoken to me, and how His mercy and goodness have followed me all the days of my life. I find this practice encouraging and life-giving.

About a year ago, I happened to come across my journal from a time when my children were in elementary school. I read an entry that shocked me! It was a conversation my daughter shared with me expressing her desire to someday serve as a missionary in India. I had long forgotten that conversation. But today, she is serving as a missionary in India!

Throughout the Scriptures, the Lord is always encouraging His people to remember (and re-visit) Who He is, and what He has done. Personally, I have found that recording and remembering what He has done in the past, gives me a broader perspective of my life, and increases my faith as I look to the future.

Let's remember, the Israelites built altars of stones to remember the things that God had said to them and done for them. Journaling is taking time to assemble stones of remembrance in my life. I can go back through the pages of my journey and see the ways I have grown and His "fingerprints" of faithfulness and love to me. I can re-visit moments of intimacy with the Shepherd of my soul, the mountain peaks, the difficult valleys, the ordinary days...*Immanuel, the Lord, **with** me!*

HIS LOVE FOR ME

An Excerpt from My Own Journal on God's Personal Love for Me

These reflections came out of a season of my life when I needed to focus my mind on God's love for me. I journaled through Scripture on God's character, and then personalized it with my name. You could do the same and even add to this list. I framed it and placed it beside my bed for morning and evening meditation.

I have chosen you, you are My beloved. – Ephesians 1:11

You are Mine, My child. – I John 3:1

I have called you by your name. – John 10:3, Isaiah 43:10

I made you wonderful. ("I praise You because I am wonderfully made.")
    – Psalm 139:14

*You were My original creation, for I created your inmost being and knit you
    together in your mother's womb.*
    – Psalm 139:13

I am familiar with all your personal ways and know your thoughts.
    – Psalm 139:3

*As a mother who cannot forget her nursing baby, even so much greater is
    My love for you. I will never forget you.* – Isaiah 49:15

I have engraved you on the palm of My hand. – Isaiah 49:16

I even know every hair on your head. – Matthew 10:30

*I made no mistake when I made you. Your frame was not hidden from
    Me when I made you in the secret place. My eyes saw your unformed
    substance.* – Psalm 139:15

*I had a specific purpose in mind when I made you... for I have written the
    days of your life in My book before one of them came to be.*
    – Psalm 139:16

I keep a watch over your life and guide and instruct you. – Psalm 145:20

I hold you securely in My hand... you will never be plucked out.
    – John 10:37, Psalm 37:4

I will never leave you or forsake you... wherever you flee to I am with you. – Hebrews 13:5

I never grow weary or tired of you, and My understanding of you is so great that you will never fathom it. – Isaiah 40:28

I will never stop loving you, for how vast are My thoughts toward you... they outnumber the grains of sand. – Psalm 139:17, 18

I care for you... I want to take your burdens and anxieties. – I Peter 5:7, Matthew 11:28

I delight in satisfying your desires. – Psalm 145:15-19

I call you My friend. – John 15:15

Absolutely nothing will ever separate My love from you.
    – Romans 8:35-39

Though the mountains be shaken and the hills be removed, My unfailing love for you will never change. – Isaiah 54:10

You are precious and honored in my sight, and I love you, My beloved.
    – Isaiah 43:1, 4

You are My lamb, and just as a shepherd gathers the lambs in his arms and carries them close to his heart, so do I tenderly love you.
    – Isaiah 40:11

My love for you will never fail. – Lamentations 3:22

PURSUING
THE ANCIENT PATHS

This is what the Lord says:
"Stand at the crossroads and look;
ask for the ancient paths,
ask where the good way is, and walk in it,
and you will find rest for your souls.
But you said, 'We will not walk in it.'"

— Jeremiah 6:16

This passage has been like a painting on the wall of my soul that the Lord has strategically placed before me to daily behold and meditate on. As the Psalmist so beautifully shares, I too have "set my heart on pilgrimage" (Ps. 84:5). *My one destination? To know him, in this life, as deeply as I can... until I meet him face-to-face.*

But there are times my soul wanders. I get distracted and pre-occupied, led more by my feelings than my will. I detour so often from the path, arriving at dead-ends. Daily, I find myself at the crossroad of internal choices. But the Lord is continually faithful in His love to place this picture before me, calling me back to His instruction to find and walk the *good and ancient paths.*

Years ago, when I was first drawn to this passage, I was intrigued with what Jeremiah was describing. What were these "ancient paths?" Who walked them? What stories and history would they reveal? In what ways do these paths bring rest to one's soul?

As I studied further, I discovered that Jeremiah wrote this at a time when Israel had been a nation for almost one thousand years. They had come to a place of intermingling with other nations, living a lifestyle of tolerance and compromise. Similar in many ways to our current post-modern times. Jeremiah was calling his generation back to the Lord, to return to the ways of their forefathers. God had chosen *the path* Israel was to take. They were to be a holy nation, set apart. But choosing different paths, they were missing their intended destiny and mission.

Yet my people have forgotten me; they burn incense to worthless idols, which made them stumble in their ways and in the ancient paths. They made them walk in bypaths and on roads not built up.

— Jeremiah 18:15

Jeremiah cried out: *"Ask for the ancient paths!"* The word "ancient" in Hebrew is "olam," eternal, timeless, concealed, hidden...perpetual. Here's the implication: this is a path marked out from eternity for God's people to follow. This is an old and well-worn path, continually used, clearly defined, **well-marked.** A proven path with a sure destination.

These paths to be followed are the Holy Scriptures. They are paths that the spiritual fathers, saints, and apostles have walked before us. For Judah, it was the laws of Moses, sacrifices, feasts and ways of worshiping God while in the land of Canaan. These paths are perpetual, relevant to both past and future. Paths that led our forefathers, and will lead us, into the promises and blessings of God's covenants.

Sometimes, when I am weary and in need of encouragement, it is a great comfort to know that these are the proven, eternal, God-ordained paths that will bring me to that place of rest my travel weary soul so desperately needs. Through the years I have grown to long for, learn from, and seek these ancient paths as I have sought to heed Jeremiah's instructions.

Stand at the Crossroads... and Look

What comes to your mind? A traveler...a pilgrim, who comes to a crossroad, and faces a choice. To *"stand"* is to come to a full stop, and to wait. These can be times intentionally set apart, taking time to consider, think, and observe. For me, sometimes this means a personal inventory, assessing the affections of my heart. For example, "Lord, do I really desire what You desire? Am I really following the Master of my soul? Where am I right now? Where do I want to go?" There are also "spontaneous stops" throughout the day, when the Spirit interrupts, impressing my thoughts in particular ways, bringing my attention back to Him or His purposes. For example, a moment to pause and offer praise, a prompting to pray for or call a friend, an insight for a problem or circumstance, or an answer to a prayer. He initiates. He gets my attention. On the ancient path, I am ever learning how to *"stop"* and respond to His ways and whispers, whether it is about a major life direction or correction, or an assignment to release his love or wisdom to someone in need.

I am to *"look"*. To be alert, attentive. Lord, what have You been saying to me? What are You saying to me right now? What do you see in my heart? Speak, Lord, I am open.

You can apply Jeremiah's timeless exhortation as you set apart specific times with the Lord. But this practice should be cultivated as you go about ordinary activities and God-ordained assignments, continually experiencing a lifestyle of inner quietness and listening. Amy Carmichael, accomplished and admired missionary, shares this word of wisdom:

Give much time to quietness. Listen, and do not evade the slightest whisper of guidance that comes from the Holy Spirit.

She is describing *"listening prayer,"* which simply is giving attention to God. The Holy Spirit is waiting to speak to you, and gently guide you. You can learn the voice of the Spirit downloading a message into the "inbox" of your inner life. Or it may be as simple and quick as a "text message" from God's heart to yours! As you train yourself more and more in your quiet times, to stand, and to look, you will become more aware of the road signs along your personal path. Sometimes I see, or hear, "Stop!" Other times his word to me might be "yield," or "do not enter," or perhaps a warning, "wrong way," or "U-turn!" Or his word might be more gentle; "Slow down, my daughter, you're out ahead of me here!" So, here is my constant prayer: "Lord, give me an ear inclined to hear You clearly every day, and a mind open to see You traveling with me as I walk this ancient path.

Ask for the Ancient Paths

Take time to find the right path. Why, we might ask, is this ancient path called the "good path?" Because it is God's chosen way to walk in righteousness. The only path that leads to rest for our souls. We ask, and take whatever time is required, to discern the ancient path.

We ask this first of Scripture, as we study, read and meditate. We may also inquire of godly ones in our lives who have walked the old, proven paths. We ask the Lord in prayer when we want to become more familiar with His work and His ways. We remember and review what God has spoken and done for us in times past. We are intentional in learning the signposts of the ancient paths so we can discern the paths that lead us astray. Our restlessness, busyness and discontentedness—these are indicators that we are not journeying on the path designed for us.

A beautiful attribute of my Lord that I have come to appreciate so deeply through the years is that He is the *God of invitations*, always inviting me to join Him: "Come unto me...come, all who are hungry and thirsty...seek me, and you will find me...come, learn of my ways, and discover my ancient paths." It is an *invitation to the path of a deeper spiritual life of knowing our Master, where all we do comes out of the secret place of communion with **Him***.

And Walk in It...

We are not called just to stand. We are exhorted by God's prophet to walk! This takes resolve. Daily, we make secret choices to obey and step out.

Israel's response should make our hearts shudder!

We will not stop and stand and consider and ask for the ancient paths!

After just a few years, they ended up in the pains and perplexities of captivity to a foreign oppressor.

I have found that my own heart can subtly compromise, stray, and fall into self-deception. I do *not* want to repeat the errors of Israel! *For me, intentional cultivation of the inner life keeps me asking myself every day, "Where is the good way? Where is the ancient path?" That is why I have shared this booklet with you.*

As I have sought this path through the years, I find myself now living in the daily destiny God has designed for me, awakening every morning, and asking, "Lord, what assignments do you have for me today?" I am learning more and more to recognize His voice, see His fingerprints in my life, and experience His promises fulfilled in real life situations. I am learning more how to receive His inner strength, how to persevere when I grow weary and discouraged. And I am learning how to receive His unconditional acceptance, where my soul finds true rest. I find I am more deeply in touch with Immanuel, God with me, able to discover and accept more readily the surprises and mysteries of *His* ways.

My deepest prayer is that you and I would become like those who have walked the ancient paths before us, who ended strong in the faith. That *our legacy would be that each of us, in our own way, was privileged to be a part of God's history...His story, for His glory, on this earth.* And that because of our faithfulness to walk this path, no matter how difficult, narrow or less traveled it might be, generations to come would be inspired to seek, and ask, *"Where are Your ancient paths?"*

APPENDIX

In the following pages you will find some Bible Study tools to use as you are doing an in-depth study of a Scripture passage. Many of us are familiar with basic inductive study methods. Sometimes they can seem overwhelming. I hope this "Bible Study Tools" format will simplify it for you. In certain seasons of my walk I have benefitted from taking an extended time during the week to do an in-depth study. Out of that study the Lord has led me to Scriptures that I can then spend time meditating on throughout the week or month.

I'm also including a list of Scriptures and ideas for engaging meditation exercises.

BIBLE STUDY TOOLS

Exploring God's Treasure Chest through inductive study

---

1. What Does It Say?

Seeing things as they really are, not as imagined

Look for: people, events, ideas, instructions.

  who is involved?
  what do you learn about people, events, or instructions?
  when is it happening?
  where is it taking place?
  why is something said or included?
  how is it accomplished?

Look for: key words & phrases that seem to be important or repeated (circle them)

Look for:
  • a quality of God (who He is)
  • the work of God (what He does)

Look for: relationships between thoughts
  • connections:
    in order that ... a purpose
    for ... a reason
    therefore ... a result
  • compare and contrast
    (new nature/old nature)
  • logical conclusion
    (an if-then statement)

Look for:
  • a promise
  • a command
  • a sin
  • an example to follow

Look for:
  • lists of ways to pray, topics, character qualities, things to avoid, exhortations

---

2. What Does It Mean?

Ask not what the passage means to you, but what it meant to the author.

• Look up the meaning of key words you don't know.
• How does this passage relate to what comes before and to what follows?
• Use cross-references to gain insight.
• Re-read the passage and answer the question, *"What did the author mean?"*
• Summarize the author's meaning in your own words.

3. How Does It Apply to Me?

What the passage means to me, and how I need to respond;
being transformed into His image.

EXAMPLE ONE:

Your observation and personal application

A Promise:	What new truth I should believe
A Command:	What I should do; an action
A Sin to Avoid:	Where I fall short
An Example to Follow:	In my attitudes, my relationship with God, or my relationship with another
A Quality of God:	How does my understanding of who God is help me to trust Him more with my circumstances today so that I'll come to know Him better

EXAMPLE TWO:

"All Scripture is God-breathed and is useful for teaching,
reproof, correction, and training in righteousness." — 2 Timothy 3:16

Teaching:	What truth or principle did I learn from this passage? What did I learn about the Lord and His character?
Reproof:	Admitting where I'm wrong in thought or behavior
Correction:	What will I do to change? Is there something to confess to God or to another? What steps must I do today?
Training:	How can I make this truth a *consistent* part of my walk with Christ this week, so that I'll come to know Him better?

Pray through the Scripture He has highlighted for you,
and meditate on it throughout the week.

The Lord has encouraged you today;
Offer Him a heart of praise for who He is.

IDEAS FOR MEDITATION

"Meditate on [the Law] day and night"
— Joshua 1:8-9

In the imagery of Psalm 84, those who seek the Lord have "set their hearts on pilgrimage." As we meditate, may our hearts become well-worn paths towards God. And we make those paths by walking in the same place day after day. The following are Scriptures to give you focus to your times of meditation, as you develop your path by being daily in His Word.

God Revealed in the New Testament

"Jesus is the exact representation of God." — Hebrews 1:3

"I am the Good Shepherd"... Jn. 10:1-6
"The Water of Life" ....Jn. 7:37
"The Servant" .... Jn. 13:1-10
"Alpha and Omega".. Rev. 1:8
"Comforter"... Jn. 14:1-3

The Names of God

"The name of the Lord is a strong tower." — Proverbs 18:10

Every name reveals the character of God. Focus on a name of God and personalize it — e.g., "Lord, You are Jehovah Shalom, my peace, even as I find myself in confusion."

Jehovah Jireh — "Lord who provides"...................................Gen. 22:14
Jehovah Rapha — "Lord who heals"...Ps. 23
Jehovah Shalom — "The Lord our Peace" ....Jud. 6:24
Jehovah Shammah — "The Lord is Present"........................ Ezk. 48:35
Jehovah Roi — "The Lord my Shepherd" .... Ps. 23:1
El Shaddai — "Almighty God" ....Gen. 17:1
El Elyon — "Most High"..Gen. 14:18
I Am ....Jn. 8:58

The Parables of Jesus

The parables (some examples below) give us insight into our relationship with God.

The Kingdom of God (soil, mustard seed, treasure)......................Mt. 13
The friend at midnight..Lk. 11:5-8
The Good Samaritan.. Lk. 10:30-37
God's Love .... Mt. 18:12-14
Lost sheep, coin, son .... Lk. 15:8-10
Wedding feast .... Lk. 14:7-15
Wise steward.. Lk. 12:35-40

My Identity in Christ

Discovering who I am and Whose I am

A child of God ....Jn. 1:12
A friend of God..Jn. 15:15
A temple...a dwelling place of God .... 1 Cor. 3:16
A new creation... 2 Cor. 5:17
God's workmanship..Eph. 2:10
Our life hidden in God .... Col. 3:3
Chosen by God, dearly loved .... Col. 3:12

Attributes of God

Love...Deut. 7:6-10, Jer. 31:3
Omnipotent...Heb. 1:3, Ps. 62:11
Omniscient...Ps. 139:2, Ps. 90:8
Omnipresent..................Ps. 139:7, Gen. 16:13, Heb. 13:5, 1 King. 8:27
Holy ....Is. 6:3, Ex. 15:11
Sovereign .... Col. 1:15-17
Good ....Jas. 1:17, Nah. 1:7
Unchanging...................................... Heb. 13:8, Ex. 3:14, Mal. 3:6

Descriptions of God

A refuge .... Deut. 33:27
The potter ....Isa. 64:8, Isa. 45:9
A hiding place... Ps. 32:7
A rock ....Ps. 61:2, Ps. 71:3
Refiner and purifier..Mal. 3:3
Comforter.. 2 Cor. 1:3
Morning star .... Rev. 2:28
Friend..Jn. 15:13
Shepherd ....Ps. 23
Bridegroom ....Isa. 62:5

Ways of God

"I will meditate on all your works and consider *all your mighty deeds."* — Psalm 77:12

We consider what He has done so we can know Him more deeply.

Consider God's wonders ....Job. 37:14
Consider God's heavens...Ps. 8
Consider God's love...................................... Ps. 103:11-17
Consider God's handiwork...................................... Ps. 143:5

Meditate on . . .

Your favorite passages and verses

Your favorite promises

The Lord's Prayers (Mt. 6, Jn. 17)

Prayers in the Epistles (Eph. 1:17-22, Eph. 3:14-20, Col. 1:9-13)

The Fruit of the Spirit (Gal. 5:22)

The Armor of God (Eph. 6:10-18)

Some of my Special Passages

Undivided heart .... Ps. 86:11-13

If you want to see God .... Mt. 5:8, Ps. 24:3-4

Bear with one another... Col. 3:12-17

The Long Name of God... Ex. 34:6-7

Above all else, guard your heart.....................................Prov. 4:20-27

Holding onto God's peace .... Phil. 4:7-8

Knowing Christ better .... Phil. 3:7-10

God's wonderful knowledge of me .... Ps. 139:1-18

The Love chapter...1 Cor. 13

Love the Lord .... Deut. 10:12-21

What is faith ....Heb. 11:1

Nothing can separate us from His love ....Rom. 8

Loving others.. Col. 3:12-17

God's nature ....Ps. 90, 103

The Lord is my shepherd...Ps. 23

One thing to ask of God ....Ps. 27, 84

Teach us to number our days.. Ps. 90:7-12

The Lord's Prayer... Mt. 6:9-14

Trusting Him ....Josh. 1:6-9, Ps. 34, 37

God's protection .... Ps. 91, Isa. 43:1-7

Repentance ....Ps. 51

God's presence with you ....Isa. 41:10

Waiting and renewal.. Isa. 40:25-31

God's compassion...Lam. 3:23

The Ten Commandments.. Ex. 20:1-17

The power of God's Word ....Ps. 19, Heb. 4:12

Prayers in the Epistles .... Eph. 1:17-22, Eph. 3:14-20, Phil. 1:9

SUGGESTED PASSAGES FOR LECTIO DIVINA

Consider reading these in a variety of translations.

Choose a gospel account of Jesus where he engages with people. Enter into this passage meditatively, with all of your senses and God-given imagination, to personally encounter Jesus.

Exodus 34:5-7

Proverbs 4:20-27

Proverbs 8:32-36

Isaiah 30:15-18

Isaiah 43:16-21

Jeremiah 6:16, 17

Jeremiah 17:5-10

Hosea 2:14-16

Psalm 23

Psalm 27:1-6

Psalm 90:12-17

Psalm 139:1-18

Matthew 11:28-30

Mark 14:1-9

1 Corinthians 13:4-8

2 Corinthians 4:16-18

Colossians 3:12-17

Philippians 4:6-9

James 1:1-5

www.ingramcontent.com/pod-product-compliance
Lightning Source LLC
Chambersburg PA
CBHW060335050426
42449CB00011B/2763